PROFIT *or* WEALTH?

Kurt,
To your success!
Ruth King

Advance Praise for
PROFIT *or* WEALTH?

"*Profit or Wealth?* is unlike any other book. We all know about the harsh, yet valuable lessons that come from failure. *Profit or Wealth* is the best guide ever to prevent that disaster."

—**Will Ezell**, Strategic Marketing Advisor who builds revenues and profits for the *Fortune 500* and small businesses.

"Ruth King's approach to helping business owners understand the nuances of wealth and profit makes this book must reading."

—**Kevin Price**, Host of the nationally syndicated Price of Business radio show.

"*Profit or Wealth*? did something surprising. It gave me what I wanted, a quick, understandable and entertaining financial read, while giving me what I NEEDED in relatable, short stories.

Ruth King blends rules, facts and case studies in a way that leaves me grateful our 50-year family company can now avoid becoming a cautionary tale."

—**Tanya Dyer**, Esq., Business & Life Coach, Author, Divorce Attorney, Family Owned Earthmoving Company

"Would you like to stop working for wages in your own business? Would you like start moving toward financial independence without working harder than you do now? Do you like stories? If you answer these question in the affirmative, do not put down Ruth King's new book until you've spent at least 15 minutes inside. After 15 minutes with *Profit or Wealth?*

you'll be hooked. Like no one else, Ruth reveals in plain English the steps to take to shift from mere profitability to true wealth-building. This book will change your life. Thank you, Ruth."

—**Jim Blasingame,** Host of nationally syndicated, The Small Business Advocate Show, Author of *The Age of the Customer* and long-time admirer of Ruth King

"For over 34 years I've engaged with thousands of small businesses through speaking, consulting, and my books. One thing that's become clear is most small businesses are started by someone with a strong love and aptitude in a particular field.

It's all well and good for people to do this, but I discovered a long time ago most of these people have two big gaps in their knowledge and experience regarding running a business. For one, a successful business person MUST have a strong focus on sales and marketing. Without those, there is no business.

Equally important, a successful business person MUST have full knowledge of his/her financial picture. Most I've encountered don't. And too often, companies go out of business by not completely understanding their financials accurately— inventory, pricing, cash flow, debt management, and recurring revenue, for example.

I don't teach financials. Ruth King does. I just finished her latest book, *Profit or Wealth?* and plan to recommend it to all of my clients, BFFs, and readers. This book will teach every one of them the most important approach to successful managing and understanding their business finances.

If you have a small business, you should read this, too."

—**Steve Miller**, Kelly's Dad, Marketing Gunslinger Author of Amazon #1 Best Seller, *Uncopyable: How to Create an Unfair Advantage Over Your Competition*

"At last, a book that breaks down the potential issues and pitfalls of running a business in easy to understand examples and illustrations. *Profit or Wealth?* should be a required '*must-read*' for every contractor who built a service business based on their skill—but aren't yet truly comfortable understanding the accounting side of managing it. Ruth King's insight and knowledge gained in working with businesses for over 30 years makes this book outstanding. Not only are her rules and guidelines practical as well as easy-to-follow, her ability to use real-life situations to demonstrate their purpose drives home her points in a way anyone can understand. *Profit or Wealth?* is a great book that should be required reading for every business owner."

—**Dave Squires**, President of Contr@ctor's Online-Access, Inc.

"Many business owners get caught up in the day-to-day activities of running the business. The problem is, without a strategy to build profits and wealth, you can work for many years and end up with nothing to show for it.

The focus of *Profit or Wealth?* is on the end game. Read this book, apply the author's knowledge and many years of experience working with small businesses, and you'll methodically build a valuable business that can be sold or passed along to the next generation.

Critical accounting principles are key. You need to understand what to do, and just as important, why. The book lays it all out, and explains what you need to pay attention to on an ongoing basis. Real stories demonstrate the difference this makes—ranging from success stories to businesses who succumbed to common pitfalls with disastrous results.

Profitability is what leads to building long-term wealth. But it takes more than accounting principles—to build wealth, you must create a stream of recurring revenue. Ruth explains what that means, and how you can create this for your own business.

If you're a business owner who wants both profitability *and* wealth, read this book, implement its principles and take charge of your destiny."

—**Kay Miller**, Coach, Speaker, and
Marketing Consultant The Adventure, LLC

"Kevin O'Leary from the TV hit "Shark Tank" says there are three things you must know in order to convince him to invest. 1) You must know your business so well that you can explain what it does in less than one minute. 2) You must know what makes you different from every other similar offering in the market place and explain that convincingly in less than 30 seconds. 3) You must know your numbers and this is where almost every entrepreneur fails. But you won't if you read and study the simple yet critical concepts that Ruth lays out in this book. It's so easy to read.

I have worked exclusively with over 300 business owners over the past two decades and from now on, I won't work with them unless they read and understand what is presented in this book. If you dropped out of grade 9 you will understand it, and if you graduated with an MBA from Harvard, you will learn how to keep things simple yet effective.

There are lots of great books on management, culture, processes, accounting, vision or business planning, and I've felt that I've read them all. After 20 years working with business owners, considering every book I've ever read, I find this book to be not just a good read, but a critical handbook for the beginning entrepreneur, or financially frustrated business owner. I will be handing it out to every business owner I know. I would recommend this book over mine, because my book is on how to manage people, but if don't read and execute on everything that Ruth says in this masterpiece, you won't have people to manage.

They say that "pornography" is difficult to define, but you know it when you see it. That's the way I felt about accounting and finance concepts until I read this book. Now I can explain things in one sentence so that the person I'm speaking with can understand. This book is brilliant!"

—**Kevin G. Armstrong**, Best Selling Author, *The Miracle Manager: why true leaders rarely make great managers*, Small Business Advisor, and Chief Disruptor at The Interdependent Training Group.

PROFIT *or* WEALTH?

SIMPLE RULES
FOR SUSTAINABLE
BUSINESS GROWTH

RUTH KING

NEW YORK

LONDON • NASHVILLE • MELBOURNE • VANCOUVER

PROFIT *or* WEALTH?
SIMPLE RULES FOR SUSTAINABLE BUSINESS GROWTH

Published in New York, New York, by Morgan James Publishing. Morgan James is a trademark of Morgan James, LLC. www.MorganJamesPublishing.com

State and local laws vary significantly and it is the responsibility of the user of this book to ensure that the activities suggested in this book comply with all laws that apply to the employers, readers, and users of this book's operations.

Profit or Wealth? Simple Rules for Sustainable Business Growth is designed to educate and provide general information regarding the subject matter covered. However, state and local laws and practices vary from state to state and are subject to change. Because each reader and company is different and each situation in that company is different, specific advice should be tailored to that particular company and circumstances. For this reason, the reader is advised to consult with his or her own advisors regarding the individual specific situation.

The author has taken reasonable precautions in the research for and writing of this book and believes that the facts presented in the book are accurate as of the date written. However, neither the author nor the publisher assume any responsibility for any errors or omissions. The author and publisher specifically disclaim any liability resulting from the use or application of the information contained in this book, and the information is not intended to serve as legal advice or financial advice related to individual situations.

ISBN 978-1-64279-939-2 paperback
ISBN 978-1-64279-940-8 eBook
Library of Congress Control Number: 2019919323

Cover Design by:
Rachel Lopez
www.r2cdesign.com

Morgan James is a proud partner of Habitat for Humanity Peninsula and Greater Williamsburg. Partners in building since 2006.

Get involved today! Visit
www.MorganJamesBuilds.com

This book is dedicated to the millions of hardworking small business owners. May the rules of profit and wealth give you the tools to create profit and wealth in your business and your life.

TABLE OF CONTENTS

Read This First — *xiii*

Introduction — *xvii*

Don't Grow Unless You Are Willing to Do These Two Things — **1**

Bookkeeper's and Owner's Responsibilities in the Creation of Profit and Wealth — **7**

Did You Buy a Job? — **13**

Profit Rules — **15**

  1: Live, Eat, and Breathe Net Profit per Hour — 15

  2: Know Your True Costs — 21

  3: Price for Profit — 26

  4: Ensure Consistent Monthly Gross Margins — 30

  5: Ensure Continuous Profits — 40

  6: Build Recurring Revenue from a Profit and Loss Perspective — 42

  7: Understand That Profits and Cash Are Not the Same — 49

  8: Review Timely, Accurate Financial Statements Each Month — 51

  9: Understand That Inventory Is a Bet — 56

  10: You Can't Take a Percentage to the Bank — 59

Wealth Rules	**63**
1: Pay Attention to Your Balance Sheet	63
2: Separate Business Expenses from Personal Expenses	68
3: Build Recurring Revenue from a Wealth Perspective	71
4: Build a Great Culture That Is Not Dependent on You	73
5: Monitor Your Cash	76
6: Save Cash	80
7: Have a Sound Collection Policy	85
A Note before Reading and Applying Wealth Rules 8–10	87
8: Have a Sound Inventory Policy	87
9: Have a Sound Debt Policy	90
10: Have an Increasing Current Ratio	93
Implementing the Profit and Wealth Rules	**97**
Zoe's Story	98
Ted's Story	103
Leo's Story	108
Samantha's Story	112
Julie and John's Story	116
Conclusion	**121**
Acknowledgments	*123*
About the Author	*125*
A Special Offer	*129*

READ THIS FIRST

Jim and Mark each own and operate a restaurant.

Jim had a great weekend. The restaurant revenues were among the highest they had ever had. He was thrilled with the profitable weekend. Unfortunately, Jim didn't really know who was dining in the restaurant. He did not instruct and train his staff to get the names of the diners, birthdays, or other pertinent information to turn those diners into returning customers. He *hoped* that he would have another busy, profitable weekend.

Mark also had a great weekend. The restaurant revenues were among the highest they had ever had. They added 15 new diners to their frequent diner program (i.e., recurring revenue customers). Servers asked for and received these diners' names, birthdays, and anniversaries and a physical and an email address where they could contact them. These 15 new diners would be sent emails and postcards that gave them a reason to return to the restaurant. These marketing communications were special invitations only for their preferred customers and included a free entrée or dessert on their anniversaries and birthdays. Mark also planned special events only for program members throughout the year to ensure that there would be diners in his restaurant.

Mark knew that he would have many more profitable weekends. He knew his customers. He sent them marketing messages giving them a reason to return. And, from experience, he knew the percentage that would return and bring potential new restaurant diners.

Which of these two restaurant owners really had a great weekend? Mark. He built profit *and* wealth.

Now, the stories of two contractors, Paul and George:

Paul and George were located in different cities. Their companies were similar in size, each generating over $5 million in revenues. Both contractors had 10 profitable years. Paul was thrilled with his profits over the 10 years. He saved his money and built his maintenance base (i.e., recurring revenue customers). Paul and his team grew maintenance customers and cash.

George was also thrilled with his profits over the 10 years. He relied on the great economic times and didn't focus on building his recurring revenue maintenance base. In addition, those 10 profitable years gave him great vacations, great second homes, and other "big boy toys." George turned the profits into cash and spent the cash. He didn't save any money.

The economy tanked. Paul, who had built wealth (i.e., recurring customer revenue and cash savings), survived the downturn. It was a rough two years. The company had to cut costs and use some of the cash that they had saved to survive. Most of the recurring revenue customers remained customers. These customers saw the value in their maintenance program since they saved money on utility bills and repairs.

George also had a rough two years. The company didn't have a recurring revenue base to survive, nor did it have the cash to survive the two years. The company filed for bankruptcy at the end of the first year and went out of business, even though they had been a company with more than $5 million in revenues. The company didn't have the wealth to survive the downturn.

A great weekend, month, or year should be defined not only by profits but also by how many new recurring revenue customers you added *and* retained. Recurring revenue customers are your future wealth and future profits. The more recurring revenue customers you have and retain, the wealthier your company is.

There will always be economic ups and downs. Building profits and wealth is critical for survival. Profit and wealth are also critical to achieve your end game—whether it is to sell the business, turn it over to employees, or keep it running forever.

INTRODUCTION

Which do you want, profit or wealth?

The answer, as you will discover in this book, is that you need—and should want—both. From a business perspective, you cannot have wealth without profits. Many books have been written about how to generate personal wealth. This book deals with business wealth. If your business is to survive and give you something worth selling or passing along to the next generation, you need both business profit and business wealth.

The purpose of your business is to profitably take care of your customers. Taking care of your customers is not enough. If you don't earn a profit, you will eventually go out of business, draining what wealth you may have had before you started your company.

Business profit is built through the profit and loss (also called P&L) statement. Business wealth is built through the balance sheet. Many small business owners only pay attention to building profit and ignore the wealth-building balance sheet. You have to pay attention to both for long-term survival.

I have been helping small businesses grow profitably and build wealth since 1981. Over the years I have witnessed and helped many companies who got into trouble financially. They got into trouble because they grew and never looked at a profit and loss statement or a balance sheet. They had no clue what their expenses really were and whether the company was making a profit. The only thing they knew was if they had cash in the bank. These owners grew without paying attention to their financial statements. Only when they got into cash trouble did they try to figure out what went wrong.

Often these owners are shocked that they are losing money and have been for years, without knowing it. How can this be? By paying attention only to the cash that is in their bank account rather than whether the products and services they produce actually are profitable.

Growth masks losses. As long as there is increasing cash in the bank from increasing sales, you are lulled into a state of bliss. Then, when growth stops or revenue decreases, the reality of no profit comes crashing into your life. You can't meet payroll or pay a vendor or take discounts on payables. You can't imagine what is wrong. What's wrong? Sales that are not profitable for many years.

Here is Alex's story:

Alex was tired of working for his current employer. He thought he could do better and started his own business. The business rapidly grew to over $3 million in five years. Unfortunately, Alex never looked at his financial statements and relied only on the amount of cash in the bank to determine how well he was doing. He started having cash flow problems because of a project that went highly over budget and "ate cash"; then he got help analyzing his financial statements. Alex discovered that most of his projects were unprofitable. He was "turning cash"—that is, the payments for a finished project paid for start-up of the next project. As long as the company grew, there was always sufficient cash to fund the projects. With this large loss, he was in a severe cash shortage, and the business may not survive.

Here is Peter's story, another way profitable companies can go out of business:

Peter owned a very profitable business for more than 10 years. He built it from scratch to over $5 million in revenues. One week, three of the company's major customers filed bankruptcy, leaving Peter with over $1 million in receivables that he couldn't collect. Peter had already paid his suppliers and employees for the work that was billed. So, the company lost the revenue and paid the expenses against the revenue. Over the years,

Peter hadn't saved enough cash to cover the $1 million shortfall and expenses, even though his company was very profitable. This caused severe cash flow problems that the company couldn't recover from. Peter's company went out of business.

Really smart business owners pay attention to their profit and loss statements and balance sheets from the day they start their businesses. They learn what they mean and how to make good business decisions using those statements. They build profit and wealth.

Here is Will and Justin's story:

Will and Justin bought the business they worked in. It had less than $750,000 in revenues. They knew how to do the work. They did not know how to run a business. I helped them build the business's profit and wealth over the next 16 years.

In year 15 of our working relationship, Will and Justin decided that they wanted to sell the business and started looking for a buyer. In the business's 16th year, Will and Justin sold the business for more than $9 million in cash.

Yes, it was profitable. However, the new owners were just as concerned about the customer base they built as they were about the business profits. The customer base was where the wealth and return on investment for the new owners really was.

Profit or Wealth? Simple Rules for Sustainable Business Growth gives you Profit Rules and Wealth Rules to implement so you achieve business success. These rules may seem difficult at first. They may present a totally different way of thinking than you are used to. As you implement these rules and continue along the profit and wealth path, you'll find that these rules give you the freedom to achieve what you desire.

The names of the business owners in the stories I write about in this book have been changed. In addition, some of the locations have been changed to protect the privacy of the company owners.

This introduction ends with an overview of cash vs. accrual accounting, profit and loss statements, and balance sheets since I will be referring to them throughout the book. Detailed information about these accounting terms can be found in my book *The Courage to be Profitable: Get and Stay Profitable in Less than 30 Minutes a Month.*

What Is Cash vs. Accrual Accounting?

Cash basis accounting recognizes revenue (i.e., a sale) when you get the cash in the door. It recognizes expenses when you pay the expense. There are no accounts receivable, accounts payable, or inventory.

Accrual accounting recognizes revenue when you send the invoice to your customer, whether or not you have gotten paid. It recognizes an expense when you receive the bill from a supplier, whether or not you have paid the bill. There are accounts receivable, accounts payable, and inventory.

You must operate your business on an accrual basis so that you have consistent profit and loss statements (see Profit Rules 2 and 4). Depending on the advice of your CPA, you might pay your taxes on a cash basis.

What Are Profit and Loss Statements?

Profit and loss statements tell you whether your company earned a profit for a specific period of time. They say that revenues exceeded expenses when the statement shows a positive profit number at the end. They say that expenses exceeded revenues when the statement shows a negative profit number at the end.

Your company can produce many types of revenue. Each of your products and services is responsible for a piece of total revenue and total expense. Everything your company produces must at least break even. Small businesses cannot afford "loss leaders" for long.

There are also two types of tangible expenses: direct expenses, also known as cost of goods sold expenses, and overhead or general and administrative expenses.

Cost of goods sold expenses occur when you sell something. Overhead expenses are incurred whether or not you sell a dollar's worth of product. These are the costs that you incur just to stay in business.

What Are Balance Sheets?

Balance sheets are called balance sheets because assets must equal liabilities and net worth (also called equity or capital). Your company's balance sheet started the day you started your business. It will end the day the business closes its doors.

Your balance sheet gives you the company's long-term profitability and lets you know if you are heading for a cash flow issue, if the company can pay its bills, or if it is burdening itself with too much growing debt.

Your balance sheet shows the wealth of your company.

Don't Grow Unless You Are Willing to Do These Two Things

||||||||||||||||||||||||||||||||||||||||||||||||||||||||||||||||||||||||||||||||||||||||

I see many business owners get into financial trouble when they grow. Doing these two things helps avoid major catastrophes. If you don't do these two things, it's not *if* your business will get in trouble, it's *when* your business *will* get into trouble.

1. Review Timely, Accurate Financial Statements Each Month

No one, unless they are a bookkeeper or CPA, starts a business to perform the financial functions of business. We start because we see a need, we want to satisfy a dream, or a hobby turns into a business—not because we want to do the books.

When your company is small, you can control everything. You know that all of the customer invoices have gone out because you sent them. You know when you get paid because you are the person going to the bank. You know when the supplier bills come in because you get the mail and you write the checks. You don't pay attention to pricing and profit as long as there is cash in the checking account. You rarely, if ever, print out the company's financial statements. You don't need to, you think, since you have a finger on everything that is happening with your business.

Then, the company grows. You can no longer sell, produce the products and services, manage employees, take care of customers, and do the bookkeeping on your own. You hire people to help you. One of the first people you usually hire is a bookkeeper. You breathe a sigh of relief because you no longer have to deal with the bookkeeping. You hated it and didn't pay attention to it except at tax time, when you handed your CPA your QuickBooks or other accounting information…which probably wasn't correct.

If your spouse volunteers to do the bookkeeping and they don't have any bookkeeping background, they should take a bookkeeping course. Otherwise, your spouse will muddle through the books, making guesses and mistakes and producing financial statements that are probably wrong and cannot be relied on.

Then a cash crunch hits, or you get an IRS notice, and the arguments begin at home and in the office. I've seen too many divorces because a spouse who had no idea what they were doing dealt with the books.

Even if you hire a bookkeeper, you cannot abdicate the review of monthly financial statements. *Profit or Wealth?* gives you an overview of how to interpret balance sheets and profit and loss statements. My book *The Courage to Be Profitable* gives you a detailed financial explanation, in English rather than in accounting babble.

Learning to understand your financial statements will keep you abreast of the financial areas of your business. They help you spot minor issues before they become major crises so you can resolve them before a catastrophe hits and potentially causes bankruptcy.

Financial statements are not rocket science. They are simply understanding a few accounting terms and performing a little addition, subtraction, multiplication, and division. Today's bookkeeping is not like the arduous and meticulous ledger books of the 1940s or like the ancient Chinese, who added on an abacus! You can use an accounting software program and a calculator.

You've probably done harder things in your life and succeeded. Think about the process that you used to learn the production part of your business or a hobby. It took practice to get it right. You were willing to commit to the practice because you wanted a result.

Commit to investing 30 minutes a month on your financial statements. Within a few months you will be understanding them with ease and wonder why you ever thought they were so hard.

2. Report Accurate Inventory on the Company's Balance Sheet Each Month

This section does not apply to those companies that have no inventory. But for those companies who do have inventory, it is critical to know how much the company has at all times because inventory is a bet (see Profit Rule 9).

I have seen too many balance sheets with no inventory or the same inventory value each month. If your company uses inventory to produce products and services, it changes on a monthly basis because your sales change on a monthly basis.

If there is no inventory or the same inventory value on your company's balance sheet, then your profit and loss statement shows less profit than it should. Why? Because all materials purchased are expensed as cost of goods sold. Some of those materials are actually not a part of cost of goods sold because they are sitting on a shelf or in an employee's truck. The only time a part should be accounted for in cost of goods sold is when it is used to produce a product or a service.

Putting inventory on your balance sheet and properly accounting for it is painful at first, especially if your company has grown to $1 million or more in revenues. Many accounting software programs can help you track inventory properly. In addition, barcoding has made it easier to account for materials going into your company and being used to produce products and services.

Here is Mike's story:

Mike was the CEO of a $6 million company when I started working with him. I realized that the company had not performed a physical inventory count in two years. I saw employees taking materials for jobs they were doing without letting anyone know what they were taking. There was no inventory control. The balance sheet said that the company had about $500,000 in inventory. I knew this was wrong simply by looking at what materials were in the warehouse.

After many conversations, Mike finally agreed to have the inventory counted. After it was counted, the company had about $250,000 in inventory. The balance sheet said $500,000 in inventory, so the company lost $250,000 in value in one day! It was a shock to Mike.

Then we did the math. A $250,000 loss in two years was $125,000 per year or approximately $2,400 per week. With 30 employees who use inventory on their jobs, this was only $80 per week or $16 per day in losses. That was easy to do, since many of the parts cost more than $25 each.

Things changed quickly. Material was tracked, and as a result, revenues and profits increased because all materials were billed to the customer. In addition, unnecessary inventory purchases decreased, which increased cash flow.

If your company is smaller and you only have $10,000 in inventory, make sure that inventory is accounted for and tracked. A $500 loss in inventory hurts the company's bottom line as significantly as a $250,000 loss in inventory in a larger company.

Bookkeeper's and Owner's Responsibilities in the Creation of Profit and Wealth

||||||||||||||||||||||||||||||||||||||||||||||||||||||||||||||||||||||||||||||||||||

If you have a bookkeeper who supposedly knows what they are doing and your books are a mess, the first question to ask is, "Why?" If a bookkeeper knows what he or she is doing, your books should clean. They should be readable. If they are a mess, then you may have an embezzler. By keeping the books a mess, the embezzler can easily hide his or her actions. You can't follow what's going on in your business, so you probably won't catch the embezzlement.

If you decide to get an audit or have someone like me look at your financial procedures and financial statements, then don't be surprised when the embezzler strongly objects to an outsider reviewing the books, or if when an outsider does come in, the bookkeeper quits—usually with a flimsy excuse.

Many owners, once they have a bookkeeper, totally abdicate the responsibility for the financial segment of their business. As long as there is enough cash, they think they are OK. Many times they are not.

You can delegate responsibility for day-to-day bookkeeping activities. You cannot abdicate responsibility for reviewing the statements each month. When you take the time (usually less than 30 minutes a month) to review your financial statements, you'll know if something doesn't look right or the statements don't seem right. Start digging and question the entries. Ask for backup to make sure the values are correct. It's your business. You have a right to see the backup proving the correct amounts for the entries.

Here are six rules for bookkeepers:

1. Bookkeepers do not have check signing authority. If you give a bookkeeper check signing authority, then they can write a check to whomever they want, whenever they want. They can pay personal bills with your checks. Unless desperate times occur, they probably won't. However, if they have check signing authority, they can. If I were a bookkeeper, I would not want check signing authority. If the business got in trouble and did not pay the company's payroll taxes, the IRS can request payment from anyone with check signing authority, even if that person is not a corporate officer.

2. You, as the owner, are the only person who can add vendors to your accounting software. If a bookkeeper can add vendors, then they can add, say, ABC Company, a fake company with a similar name to your legitimate supplier, ABC, Inc. You sign a check to ABC

Company, thinking it is your actual vendor. After all, you saw fake invoices from and purchase orders to this company.

3. Have a payroll checking account and an operating checking account. This keeps everyone honest, not only bookkeepers. Employees only see checks from the payroll account. They don't have the checking account number for your operating account. I've seen situations where employees scanned your signature from their paycheck, stole a few checks, and embezzled thousands of dollars. By limiting the funds in a payroll account, this is less likely to occur.

4. Match the accounts payable and accounts receivable printouts with the amounts on your balance sheet. Print an aged payables and an aged receivables report. Make sure those totals match the totals on your balance sheet. If not, someone is putting journal entries in to make the balance sheet balance and may be stealing funds this way.

5. Do not accept excuses from your bookkeeper. A good bookkeeper will produce accurate, timely financial statements. If there is always an excuse as to why they are late or the financial statements are always inaccurate, then you have a problem. Good bookkeepers are mortified when they make a mistake. They pride themselves on producing timely, accurate financial statements.

6. If you are hiring a new bookkeeper, test the candidate's knowledge before you hire. People can look good on

paper and talk a good game. Give them a test to see what they really know. If you want a test that covers what a bookkeeper should know, email me at rking@ontheribbon.com. If someone doesn't pass the test, no matter how well that person presents themselves in an interview, don't hire that person!

Here is Charlie's story:

Charlie was looking for a bookkeeper to replace his current bookkeeper, who was leaving the company on good terms. One of the people he interviewed had 20 years of experience on her resume and seemed to have performed everything that would be required at his company.

When he gave her the test, she missed 12 out of 25 questions. He was shocked that someone who should have been able to pass the test couldn't.

I explained to him that even if that person had 20 years of experience, she may not understand bookkeeping, since all of the processes and procedures were already set up and she just had to step into what was previously set up properly.

Trust your gut. If you feel something is wrong and things don't make sense, then something probably *is* wrong. Most times we don't want to believe that someone we hired cannot do the job or, worse, is stealing from us. However, unfortunately it happens to hardworking business owners all the time.

In summary, your bookkeeper is responsible for producing timely, accurate financial statements, and you, as the owner, are responsible for reviewing those financial statements and making good business decisions based, in part, on what those financial statements are telling you.

Did You Buy a Job?

||||||||||||||||||||||||||||||||||||||||||||||||||||||||||||||||||||||||||||||||||||||||

Many people start businesses because they want freedom from their boss. They think, *I can do it better.* Then they go out on their own and work really hard.

Here is Frank's story:

Frank was tired of working for the company he was employed by. He wanted to quit and start his business, so he did. Frank put in long hours and didn't make a lot of profit. He did everything himself and rarely took time off. He became a slave to his business. Forty years later he was tired and wanted to sell his business.

I valued it for him. To his dismay and mine, he had almost nothing of value in his business. Frank worked hard for 40 years with almost nothing of value built in those years of hard labor.

Frank bought a job for 40 years. He never built wealth to have something to sell so he could retire.

Contrast Frank's story with Philip's story:

Philip started a business with the intention of selling it in 10 years. The team he hired were people who could potentially own the business in 10 years. He created and built a recurring revenue program. Philip saved the money he received from recurring revenue customers. The expenses from that program were funded from his profitable business. Within 10 years he had saved more than $1 million.

He sold the business to his managers and retired. He took his wealth, moved, and is living happily in another state.

Just working hard for any number of years buys you a job. Yes, you might not have a boss in the traditional sense when you own your own business. Your business just has a slave—you—if you don't build wealth.

You don't have to have employees to build wealth. Find a way to build profit and wealth, with recurring revenue and cash. Then you are not a slave to your business and have options when it is time to sell the business or retire.

Profit Rules

||||||||||||||||||||||||||||||||||||||||||||||||||||||||||||||||||||||||||||||||||

B usiness profits are required before you build wealth. These
10 rules help ensure you generate profits.

Profit Rule 1: Live, Eat, and Breathe Net Profit per Hour

Most business owners look at their profit and loss statements
by looking at the percentages. They determine a good or bad
month/year by that percentage.

For example: "Our company made a 10% net last year.
Industry average is 5% net profit. We did really well." Did you?

Percentages don't tell the real story. You can't take a
percentage to the bank. The only thing you can take to the
bank are dollars. When you manage your company's operations
by net profit per hour rather than percentages, you determine
true cost and true profit.

If you track by net profit percentage, you're fooling yourself. Why? The first thing you usually do is convert the percentage into dollars and decide whether those dollars are enough. You *must* dig deeper. What do those dollars represent? How many billable or revenue-producing hours were used to create those dollars? Then, decide whether those dollars are enough.

Jeremy and Josh meet at an industry conference. They start talking about their profits. They discover that each has a 10% net profit. Jeremy is a student of net profit per hour and explains it to Josh. Jeremy's net profit per hour is $50 per hour. When Josh does his calculation his net profit per hour is only $10 per hour. Both have the same net profit percentage. Jeremy is five times more profitable than Josh.

The percentages don't matter. The profit dollars matter. The net profit per hour matters more.

So how do you calculate net profit per hour? This is covered in detail in Profit Rule 3.

All net profit per hour pricing follows the profit and loss statement format:

> Revenue
> − Cost of Sales
> ------------------
> = Gross Profit
> − Overhead
> ------------------
> = Net Operating Profit

Adding your company's desired net operating profit per hour and the overhead cost per hour times the number of hours the job or project takes gives gross profit. Add the cost of sales to the gross profit to determine the revenue or the price to the customer.

Net profit per hour is the profit generated for each billable (i.e., revenue-producing) hour.

It is defined as:

$$\text{Net Profit per Hour} = \frac{\text{Total Net Operating Profit}}{\text{Billable Hours}}$$

Overhead cost per hour is the overhead you must cover for each billable (i.e., revenue-producing) hour.

It is defined as:

$$\text{Overhead Cost per Hour} = \frac{\text{Total Overhead}}{\text{Billable Hours}}$$

Determine how many billable hours your company had last year. This is the number of hours that were billed to a customer, the number of hours that were spent producing products and services, or both. It does not include holidays, vacations, meeting hours, training hours, or hours they were paid for other non-billable activities.

Get last year's total overhead and net operating profit (i.e., net profit before other income, other expenses, and taxes) from your profit and loss statement. Put them in the formulas above to calculate your overhead cost per hour and net profit per hour.

If your company had a loss last year, the company *paid* its customers to provide the products and services it sold to them.

The next thing to realize is that gross margins (gross profit divided by sales) don't matter. Here's why:

Table 1 is a list of 20 jobs from a client.

The abbreviations at the top of the chart are defined as follows:

- Customer names are initials to protect their identity.
- Selling price is the price the customer paid.
- GP is gross profit.
- GM is gross margin.
- OH/hr. is overhead cost per hour.
- # hours is the number of hours that job took according to payroll time sheets.
- Net profit is gross profit minus overhead. Overhead is calculated by multiplying the overhead cost per hour times the number of hours.
- Net profit per hour is net profit divided by the number of job hours.

Table 1

Customer	Sell Price	GP	GM	OH/hr	# hrs	Net Profit	Net Profit/hr
JE	12,903	5,227	40.51%	60.20	39.00	2,879	73.34
RP	11,293	4,918	43.55%	60.20	53.50	1,697	31.11
MC	13,248	5,119	38.64%	60.20	48.50	2,199	45.33
CF	15,078	7,075	46.92%	60.20	38.00	4,787	125.09
EK	9,686	4,495	46.41%	60.20	49.50	1,515	30.42

IR	23,752	11,809	49.72%	60.20	81.50	6,903	84.67
GP	3,948	2,489	63.04%	60.20	25.00	984	39.96
HT	5,644	2,273	40.27%	60.20	59.00	-1,279	-21.37
DT	11,020	4,971	45.11%	60.20	72.00	637	8.11
RR	12,082	6,499	53.79%	60.20	54.00	3,248	60.20
KP	10,363	4,991	48.16%	60.20	32.75	3,019	92.85
HG	16,620	6,852	41.23%	60.20	103.00	652	6.03
DP	30,352	11,713	38.59%	60.20	150.00	2,683	17.50
DG	2,519	1,625	64.50%	60.20	14.75	737	49.49
DH	8,534	4,337	50.82%	60.20	54.00	1,086	20.13
LP	8,822	1,712	19.41%	60.20	15.25	794	52.00
ML	7,489	3,809	50.86%	60.20	39.00	1,461	37.91
RT	8,545	4,390	51.38%	60.20	30.25	2,569	84.58
RS	10,931	3,559	32.56%	60.20	90.00	-1,859	-20.11
TJ	9,868	3,911	39.63%	60.20	60.00	299	4.68

Here's why gross margins don't matter:

The job for customer JE achieved a 40.51% gross margin and a $73.34 net profit per hour.

The job for customer HT achieved a 40.27% gross margin and lost $21.37 per hour.

These two jobs had almost identical gross margins. One achieved a net profit. The other lost a significant amount of money.

Here's another reason gross margins don't matter: The job for customer LP had a gross margin of "only" 19.41%, the lowest gross margin on the chart. Many company managers would think this job lost money. Yet, it earned a $52 net profit per hour.

The job for customer DG had the highest gross margin on the chart, 64.50%. It achieved a net profit per hour of $49.49. This net profit per hour is less than the net profit per hour of customer LP, with only a 19.41% gross margin.

This is why gross margins don't matter. The dollars do.

Determine your company's overhead and net profit per hour. This is your true profit, based on your true revenues and expenses. Percentages don't matter. Dollars do.

What net profit per hour should I earn? Many company owners have asked me this question. I never answer it. Why? Because the net profit per hour you want to earn is up to you. It is your company. It is your bottom line.

Here is Jonathan's story:

When I asked Jonathan what net profit per hour he wanted to earn, he gave me the "deer in the headlights" stare. He said, "I have no idea. I've never thought about it."

"Give me a number to start with so that we can make sure we are pricing according to the bottom line you want."

"How about $20 per hour?"

"If that is what you want, then fine. We'll start pricing using this net profit per hour."

A month later I got an email from Jonathan. It said, "Is $100 net profit per hour too piggish?"

My reply was "No. Why?"

"I did a job that did really well and earned over $100 net profit per hour. I was able to donate a portion of the profit of that job to my favorite charity. It made me feel really good."

Over the weeks and months Jonathan kept the pricing at $100 per hour or more. He was able to give more money to his favorite charities. One day, as we were discussing his pricing, I said, "You finally get it. The more you earn, the more you can give to your employees in the form of raises, training, and bonuses. And you can give more to charitable organizations."

So, what net profit per hour do you want to earn? Most company owners are not happy with a net profit per hour less than $10, because that is what you could earn working for a fast food restaurant.

First, determine what your net profit per hour is now. If you like the number, then strive to achieve it constantly. If you don't like the number, plan to raise it through increasing sales, increasing productivity of your billable or revenue-producing employees, or decreasing expenses.

Profit Rule 2: Know Your True Costs

When you understand and track all of your costs, you can make decisions about whether the costs are too high, acceptable, or too low. If a cost is too high or too low, determine why. You might have estimated incorrectly, or there may be a problem that must be resolved.

There are four types of costs:

1. Direct
2. Indirect
3. Tangible
4. Intangible

Direct costs, also called cost of goods sold, are costs you incur because you sold something. If you don't sell, you don't incur these costs. Direct costs usually include labor used to create and produce jobs/projects/widgets, equipment, materials, commissions, warranty, freight, subcontractors, and other costs you have because you sold something.

Labor cost can be tricky. Only the job labor goes in direct cost. Vacations, holidays, meeting time, and other unapplied time is an overhead expense. You can't bill for this time. Yet, you pay your employees for it. Some owners put payroll taxes for the direct labor employees in direct cost. It doesn't matter where you put it, as long as you are consistent from month to month.

Commissions are always included in direct cost. No sale, no commission. If you pay a salesperson a salary plus commission, that salary expense goes in overhead.

Indirect costs (also called overhead costs) are all of the costs you incur to stay in business. You have these costs whether or not you produce revenues. These include marketing/advertising, rent, utilities, office salaries, travel, professional fees, etc.

Tangible costs are costs that you can see. These are the costs that you write checks for. They include the direct and indirect costs for your business.

Intangible costs are the most dangerous types of costs because they are "hidden" and can dramatically affect your profitability. One typical intangible cost is sales cost. Owners accept a lot of intangible sales cost. If your salesperson's closing ratio is 25%, they are "burning" three out of four leads. How much do those leads cost? Is burning 3 out of 4 acceptable?

Lead cost includes all marketing and advertising, including referral costs, web costs, social media costs, and traditional advertising costs such as radio, television, and newspaper. Track the number of leads generated from these types of media. It's as simple as asking, "How did you hear about us?" when a new customer calls or "What prompted you to call us today?" for a customer in your database. Most software packages can track this for you. It's as simple as putting in the data.

Look at sales closing rate from a profitability perspective. Assume these facts:

- Your average sale is $10,000.
- Your desired net profit per hour is $100.
- It takes 20 hours of labor to produce the work. Look at the sales closing ratio from a profitability perspective.
- Salespeople are given 500 leads a year (10 leads a week for 50 weeks). One salesperson's closing rate is 25%. The other salesperson's closing rate is 50%.
- The company generates 125 closed jobs from salesperson 1 and 250 closed jobs from salesperson 2.

With these assumptions, the average net profit per hour for each sale is $2,000.

Salesperson 1 has a closing ratio of 25%. This means he closes 125 sales per year, generating $250,000 in net profit for your company.

Salesperson 2 has a closing ratio of 50%. This means he closes 250 sales per year, generating $500,000 in net profit for your company.

Are you willing to accept the $250,000 in intangible cost that salesperson 1 is costing your company?

If your answer was no—and it should be no—then you have two options: Train salesperson 1 so that his closing ratio increases or send him through your "career redevelopment program" (i.e., fire him).

The other major intangible costs are warranty and callback/rework expenses. For companies that produce widgets, even if you expense a small percentage of material cost for every widget and put it on the balance sheet as accrued warranty expenses to cover the inevitable warranty costs, the amount on your balance sheet is not your true warranty cost.

When a warranty call or callback occurs, a service department employee usually resolves the issue. That employee's labor cost is taken from the warranty reserve on the balance sheet and transferred to warranty revenue on the profit and loss statement. Unfortunately, this is not the only cost. There is the overhead cost to perform that work. Most companies don't consider this overhead cost when transferring funds from the warranty reserve. None that I know will let the service department get a profit on warranty expense. As a result, the service department loses the amount of profit they could have generated to resolve a paying customer's service problem.

Rework occurs when a customer is not happy with the work that your company performed. You redo it and make it right for the customer at no additional cost to the customer.

You have costs to redo the work. This causes increased expenses with no revenue to offset it. Sometimes these expenses are labor only (e.g., rewriting a marketing plan), and sometimes these expenses are for replacing defective materials.

Even if you add a small percentage of labor or material cost for every project and put it on the balance sheet as accrued warranty expenses (or warranty reserve) to cover the inevitable warranty costs, the amount on your balance sheet is not your true warranty cost.

When your company bills a manufacturer for a part that has failed, they give you a labor rate that never covers all of your intangible costs. Manufacturers don't consider overhead and profit when they establish the labor rate they will pay.

The most expensive intangible cost your company has when it performs warranty or redoes work is lost revenue opportunity cost. Not only do you have expense of paying for the employee's time, overhead, and profit, you cannot generate revenue when performing that work. If it takes two hours to perform that warranty work, that is two hours that they cannot generate revenue.

Assume that your company's average revenue is $250 per hour and it takes two hours to perform the warranty work. Your company has lost the ability to generate $500 in revenue. Add this lost opportunity cost to the cost of the employee's time and overhead. This is your company's true warranty expense.

Some company owners also attach a small profit when calculating their warranty costs. Why would an owner attach a profit? Their thought is that if they had another company performing that warranty work, they would have to pay that company's bill, which would include all expenses and a little profit.

If you have planned for the intangible warranty costs in a warranty reserve account on your balance sheet, then make sure that these costs don't exceed what you have planned for. If they are higher, then determine why and take steps to correct the costs to get them back in line.

Track all of your costs, tangible and intangible. Sometimes the intangible costs cause more loss of profit (e.g., sales closing ratios) than the tangible costs.

Profit Rule 3: Price for Profit

Pricing for real profit uses the net profit per hour methodology. Unfortunately, some business owners price by figuring out what their competitors are charging and making their pricing a little less. This is insane. How do they know their competitor is covering all of his costs? Their competitors may have economies of scale that they don't have. For example, if your competitor's overhead cost per hour is $10 less than yours, they can sell their products for less than you can and earn the same profit. Pricing your products less might mean you are losing money and your competitor isn't.

A sound pricing policy uses the profit and loss statement starting at net profit. When you calculate your desired sales price and your prices are higher than your competitors, find out how to create more value than your competitors. Otherwise you have to lower your desired net profit per hour.

	Net profit
+	Overhead
=	Gross Profit
+	Direct costs
=	Selling price

To price properly, estimate the number of hours it will take to complete the project/job or create the product.

Then decide the net profit per hour you want to earn.

Then add your company's overhead cost per hour.

That equals the gross profit per hour.

Multiply the gross profit per hour by the number of estimated hours to get the total gross profit.

Determine the direct costs (cost of goods sold).

Your selling price is the addition of the total gross profit and the direct costs.

Overhead Cost per Hour

Overhead cost per hour is defined as total overhead cost divided by the number of billable or revenue producing hours. It is easily calculated at the end of your fiscal year. Your profit and loss statement shows you the total overhead.

Divide that number by the billable or revenue producing hours that you had.

A billable hour is an hour that is used by you or your employees in the creation of a product or performance of a service. It does not include vacation hours, holiday hours, training/meeting hours, sick time, or other time you paid your employee for when he was not producing a product or service.

Let's price a service company's project using net profit per hour pricing.

Assume:

- It is estimated to take 20 hours to perform the project.
- The person performing it earns $25 per hour.
- Payroll taxes are included in overhead cost of $40 per hour.
- The company wants to earn $100 per hour.

What should the company charge for this project?

Net profit = $2,000 ($100 × 20).

Overhead = $800 ($40 × 20).

Direct cost = $500 ($25 × 20).

The project price is $3,300.

Let's price a widget using net profit per hour pricing.

Assume:

- It takes 12 minutes to produce one widget.
- The person producing the widget earns $12 per hour.
- The cost of the materials to produce the widget is $1.50.
- The overhead cost per hour is $15 per hour.
- The company wants to earn $25 per hour.

What should the company charge for this widget?

First, it takes 0.2 hours to produce one widget (12 minutes divided by 60 minutes)

Net profit = $5 (0.2 × $25).

Overhead = $3 (0.2 × 15).

Direct cost = $3.90 (labor is .2 × 12 = $2.40; materials are $1.50).

The widget selling price is $11.90.

If the selling price is higher than you've ever charged, then determine whether a customer would pay that price. There are thousands of books on selling that can help you with this question. It has been my experience that most people will pay for value. When they cannot determine the difference in value between two prices, they normally choose the lower price.

Here is Anna's story:

Anna operated what she thought was a good business. She did all of the billing herself and often decreased the cost to the customer thinking, *That was too much*, when she calculated what the price should be based on the work performed.

There were many months that the company wasn't profitable, and she was getting frustrated and started thinking whether all the time, stress, and effort was worth it.

Anna decided to calculate the company's overhead cost per hour and she decided the minimum net profit per hour that she would accept.

When the calculations were done, she was shocked. Anna had to raise the company's rates by $25 per hour. This was a huge number to her. Anna thought that she would lose all of the company's customers when she raised her company's rates.

Despite her fear, Anna raised the company's rates and gave the billing to her bookkeeper. This way she wouldn't see what the customers were being charged until she saw the accounts receivable reports.

The bookkeeper used the new pricing. Nothing happened. A few customers called questioning the invoices. However, the bookkeeper explained the work done, and the customers seemed satisfied.

Anna realized that the very few customers who did complain were the same customers who complained about every bill. She decided to get rid of those customers and invited them to use another company. She gave these customers a list of companies (the cheapest ones she knew with the worst reputations) who might be interested in doing work for them.

All but 1% of the customers stayed with Anna's company. Profits increased, cash flow increased, and Anna was less stressed.

Profit Rule 4: Ensure Consistent Monthly Gross Margins

Gross margin is gross profit divided by sales. Gross profit is always expressed in dollars. Gross margin is always expressed in a percentage. While gross profit can vary widely from month to month depending sales revenue, gross margin should not vary more than a few percentage points each month.

Table 2 shows the gross margins of two companies:

Table 2

Company A			
	Revenue	Gross Profit	Gross Margin
Jan	10,000	4,000	40%
Feb	20,000	8,200	41%
Mar	25,000	10,000	40%
Apr	50,000	21,000	42%
May	60,000	24,000	40%
Jun	80,000	32,000	40%
Jul	50,000	19,500	39%
Aug	50,000	20,500	41%
Sep	30,000	12,000	40%
Oct	30,000	12,300	41%
Nov	20,000	8,000	40%
Dec	10,000	3,900	39%

Company B			
	Revenue	Gross Profit	Gross Margin
Jan	10,000	2,800	28%
Feb	20,000	6,400	32%
Mar	25,000	10,000	40%
Apr	50,000	12,500	25%

May	60,000	27,000	45%
Jun	80,000	40,000	50%
Jul	50,000	20,000	40%
Aug	50,000	17,500	35%
Sep	30,000	12,600	42%
Oct	30,000	11,400	38%
Nov	20,000	6,400	32%
Dec	10,000	2,500	25%

Both companies have the same seasonality (i.e., higher and lower revenue months).

Company A's gross profit varies from month to month yet the gross margins are similar.

Company B's gross profit also varies from month to month but the gross margins vary widely. June's and July's gross margins vary by 10%. Assuming Company B is pricing its products the same way throughout the year, the gross margin variation should be similar to Company A's gross margin variation.

There are seven major reasons why your gross margin isn't consistent.

1. Financial Statement Fruit Salad

First, if your gross margin is negative that means you are selling a product for less than the product cost or you have financial statement fruit salad. No business owner intentionally buys a part for $25 and sells it for $10.

Financial fruit salad occurs when revenues are accounted for in one month and the expenses incurred producing those revenues are accounted for in another month. When you calculate your gross profit and gross margin, you match revenues and expenses. If they are in different months, you have apples combining with oranges, and you have fruit salad. You want revenues to match expenses in the same month. You do not want fruit salad. You want only apple salad. Revenues must match expenses in the same month. This helps ensure that you can make accurate decisions about your revenues and direct costs.

If you put revenues in one month and expenses in another month, then you are fooling yourself. Here's what happens: The month with the revenues and no expenses will look like a great month from a profit perspective. You will feel great about the business and might be lulled into a false sense of security. The month that has the expenses and no revenues will be a profit loser, and you might get worried about the business when it might be more profitable than you think it is. If there is a sale in one month, then the direct costs for that sale must be in the same month.

Quite frankly when I see negative gross margins or wildly swinging gross margins, I know that a bookkeeper is lazy because they haven't ensured that all revenues and expenses are in the same month. Or, they have charged all labor to cost of sales when part of paid labor is unapplied time.

To avoid financial statement fruit salad, make sure all revenues and expenses incurred producing those revenues are in the same month.

2. Inventory Accounted for as Material Expense (for Companies with Inventory)

If you do not have financial statement fruit salad, the next place to look is inventory accounted for as material expense.

Did you get a large stocking order from one of your suppliers? If so, then these materials should go into inventory and not be considered material expenses until they are used to produce the product or perform the service. If you purchase materials and equipment specifically for a project, then that material and equipment never goes into inventory. It is material expense and is subtracted from project revenue.

3. Projects Over- or Underestimated Labor and Material Expenses

Be careful when allowing employees to order their own materials for their projects. They might order five "just in case" when they need only two to perform their work. If these extra materials go into the project cost rather than inventory, your project material cost will be higher and your gross profit and gross margin will be lower.

If a project is supposed to take 40 hours and it takes 50 hours, then your gross profit and gross margins are lower than they should be. The reverse is also true. If your projects take less time than estimated, your gross profit and gross margin will be higher than estimated. Either can affect your total gross margin for the month.

Next look at the productivity of each employee.

Many software programs allow you to create a profit and loss statement for each employee. Do it. You'll find which employees are the most profitable for your company. If field employees have widely different gross margins, the company profit and loss statement will have varying gross margins.

Why do different employees have different gross margins? Why is their productivity different? Find the answers to these two questions and you'll increase the overall productivity and margin of the company. Unproductive employees are intangible costs to your company (see Profit Rule 2).

Then look at project estimates vs. actual costs. If a salesperson estimated 12 hours on a project and the project took 16 hours, then your gross margin will be lower than projected. On the positive side, if a salesperson estimated 12 hours and the project took 10 hours, then you have a higher gross margin than projected. Either way, the gross margin won't be consistent with the estimate.

Remember to estimate hours in half day groups. Estimate 4, 8, 12, 16, etc. hours for a project. Why? Those 10-hour projects magically stretch to 12 hours. Those 6-hour projects for some reason always take a day. Your employees stretch the time to fill their days. Just estimate full or half days.

The other issue you may have is salesperson time vs. reality time. This means that a salesperson estimates a project with lower hours so he can win the sale. Then, when the work is completed, the actual hours always come in over the bid hours. This means the projects are never as profitable as predicted. The only way to resolve this is when salespeople are paid on the net profit per hour of a project, not the sales.

4. Callbacks and Warranty Expenses

With callbacks (rework) and warranties you have an expense with no revenues to cover those expenses. In the case of warranties, you may recover part of the expense when you submit warranty claims to suppliers/manufacturers. In the case of reworks or callbacks, your employees didn't do the project correctly the first time. This is costly in terms of profits and customer satisfaction (see Profit Rule 2).

If you have a warranty part, then you have to make sure that the purchase of the replacement of that part is not an expense to the company. You've already expensed it once against the project; you can't expense it twice!

Warranty parts are not inventory. However, I have seen thousands of dollars just sitting in companies' warehouses when no one took the time to send back the parts. Or they don't send the parts back in the proper time frame and miss the opportunity to receive credit for those parts. Or they send them back and don't watch to see if they get the credits from the supplier or manufacturer. Warranties can make your direct expenses higher, which means a lower gross margin.

Callbacks and rework are internal mistakes. Find out why they are happening and fix the problem. Most times it is a training issue.

5. Paying Employees Overtime and the Customer Pays Normal Rates

You may have some recurring revenue customers who pay no overtime charges even in emergency situations. In these cases, even if you are paying your employees overtime, the customer is paying regular rates rather than overtime rates. You still have the same selling price to the customer. Margins are often lower by a percentage point or two because no overtime charges are being passed along. You can be busy and be less profitable because your margins are lower.

6. Recurring Revenue Sales and Expenses

Companies that have recurring revenue matching recurring expense in the same month will have consistent gross margins, and there should be no financial statement "fruit salad."

Companies where a recurring revenue sale is made in one month and the expenses to fulfill that sale are in another month will have financial statement fruit salad on their financial statements. If you account for a recurring revenue sale when the sale is made rather than when the work is performed, in months when you have sales and no work performed, your margins will be higher, and in months when you perform work, you have no revenue and all of the expenses, so your margins will be lower.

This is financial statement fruit salad for recurring revenue. When the sale is made, your company has a liability until it performs the work. This liability goes on the balance sheet. When the work for that revenue is performed, the liability goes away and the revenue is recognized on your profit and loss statement.

If you are noticing gross margins varying widely and none of the first six issues are present, then unfortunately you have number 7.

7. Theft

Theft can take many forms:

- Employees don't charge customers for materials they use on their projects.
- Double purchasing: An employee picks up two motors instead of one needed for a job and keeps the second motor.
- Parts that should be on the truck are not on the truck.
- Employees are stealing materials from the warehouse.

This is Peter's story, originally told in my book, *The Ugly Truth about Cash*.

Peter's company has a huge warehouse with about $500,000 in inventory in it at all times. His company has the revenues to support that amount of inventory, and it turns over very quickly.

Since there is so much inventory, the temptation to steal is there. So, he installed cameras in the warehouse to prevent this potential issue.

Peter knows the company job costs and tracks all purchases. He also knows the company's gross margins well. The company's accounting system and books are clean, and Peter gets a financial statement, which he reviews, once a month.

This statement also goes to an outside consultant—me—who analyzes the statements and reports back.

One month the gross margin was lower than expected. What was going on? It might have been a one-month glitch that would reverse itself the next month. In our discussions, we decided that it might be an accounting issue, and we decided to see what happened the next month. Peter never dreamed that someone was stealing materials.

The next month the gross margin was lower than it should be, too. Material purchases seemed higher than they should be. Again, Peter thought that someone was just not accounting for materials properly.

I also saw this and sent Peter an email after the second month, saying, "Someone is stealing inventory."

Peter emailed back: "No way. We have cameras in the warehouse, and I didn't see anything unusual."

It turned out that someone was stealing from Peter. The only place in the warehouse that didn't have video surveillance was right by the back door. He discovered this and put cameras at that door without telling anyone. Then Peter started watching.

One night he caught two employees taking materials out the back door and through the fence. They had cut a hole in the chain-link fence and put it back together so that someone driving by would never see it.

Peter caught them and had them arrested.

Theft is usually discovered during inventory counts when the actual inventory is much less than what it is supposed to be based on the balance sheet value. Hopefully, this is not the case in your company.

Watch your gross margins each month. Ensure they stay consistent. If not, these seven frequent occurrences should give you an idea where to look for the issues. Fix them so you can make great business decisions based on accurate financial data.

Profit Rule 5: Ensure Continuous Profits

Continuous profits are critical to long-term survival. And continuous, predictable losses do not make sense. Do something to prevent the losses!

Many company owners plan for and expect a predictable loss sometime during the year. For example, most heating and air conditioning contractors predict a slow first quarter and hope for a hot summer to make up for the losses. On the other hand, many retail companies base their entire year on a great fourth quarter holiday season.

Why would you do this? Why wouldn't a heating and air conditioning contractor put processes in place to at least break even in first quarter? Then, if the summer is not hot, the year will still be profitable. Likewise, why wouldn't a retailer put processes in place to increase revenues throughout the year rather than hope for a strong holiday season? As many experts have said, "Hope is *not* a strategy."

A break–even or positive net profit slower time of year is dependent on recurring revenue customers. Your recurring revenue customers are critical for profitability and wealth (see Wealth Rule 3).

One of the biggest keys to having a break-even or profitable slower time period is your attitude. If you sit back, do nothing, and say, "That's the way it is," then you will get what you expect. Recurring revenue customers are key. When you contact them and give them a reason to buy in the slowest season, you have a greater chance that the slower times will be at least break even and the usual busy times will be a huge bonus because you don't have to rely on a busy season for company profitability.

The major mistake I see companies make with growing recurring revenue programs is thinking that these programs are a loss leader and that the losses can be made up through other, "regular" sales. Most businesses are *not* supermarkets that advertise a phenomenal deal on milk to lure you into the store. Then, the milk is at the back of the supermarket so you see everything you might possibly need and walk out of the store with much more than milk.

Here is Martha's story:

Martha started and built a recurring revenue program at her company. Currently the company has 1,100 recurring revenue customers. Customers pay $157 per year to be a member of the company program. When we analyzed her cost of providing the service, the costs were $177. Martha's costs were $20 higher than revenues for each member. Her initial thought was, "So what; I will make up the $22,000 loss in other sales from these customers." I said, "It's not an additional $22,000; it's $22,000 divided by 8%," which was the company's average net profit. The company had to generate $275,000 just to make up for those losses.

After she got over the shock, Martha decided to raise the prices on the company maintenance program so the company would not suffer that loss.

Most business owners cannot afford a loss leader. Recurring revenue plans must at least break even after taking overhead costs into consideration.

Most companies have an unprofitable month or an unprofitable year every once in a while. However, no company should plan for a loss every year at a specific time.

Recurring revenue can provide your company with continuous profits. And continuous profits build wealth.

Profit Rule 6: Build Recurring Revenue from a Profit and Loss Perspective

Building a loyal customer base is critical for building wealth. Most customer bases are built using recurring revenue programs. These programs tie your customer to your company. You give them reasons to use your company year after year.

Your recurring revenue programs give you predictable revenues, expenses, and cash flow. This allows you to budget. Increasing your sales usually means increasing your recurring revenue customer base.

You probably have seen many recurring revenue programs, and you may be a member of some. Think about gym memberships, Sam's Club, Costco, Amazon Prime, wine clubs and other club memberships, your monthly video game subscriptions, Netflix and other movie subscriptions, home maintenance programs, and other things you buy where you pay a monthly fee that is taken out of your checking account or charged to your credit card each month, quarter, or year.

From a business perspective, you pay for many software programs on a monthly basis rather than an annual fee. The more companies that use the software program, the higher the recurring revenue to the software company.

Higher recurring revenue means more value and a higher selling price when that software company gets bought. Or, if the software company acquires other companies, the predictable cash is there to purchase the company and get new customers on the recurring revenue program.

To create your recurring revenue program, first answer these questions:

- What are your customers purchasing from you?
- How frequently are they buying?
- Can you incentivize them to buy more frequently?
- What other products and services could they be purchasing from you?
- What special products or benefits can you give your customers?
- Do any of your competitors have a recurring revenue program? If so, what is it?

Then create your program around the answers to these questions.

Almost every business can have a recurring revenue program. The recurring revenue program could be free (like the restaurant frequent diner club mentioned at the beginning of this book). It could have a cost to join or have several tiers (from free to a low investment to a higher investment with higher benefits). You might also create a "buy 10 and your 11th widget is free" or another plan. Just make sure to calculate the costs so that the 11th widget doesn't put your company out of business.

For product businesses, create a widget of the month club. For example, you might have a cake of the month club where you send a different cake each month. I've seen these programs with food items, beauty products, coffee, tea, and many more products. Generally these programs have a monthly investment.

For service businesses, create a maintenance program, paid newsletter, or special customer program.

You might have a paid newsletter with information that will help your customers on any topic that you are an expert in.

You might create a heating and air conditioning, plumbing, electrical, generator, chimney, lawn care, pest control, or other type of home maintenance program. These programs usually require an investment by the customer to perform the maintenance work. Just ensure that your company at least breaks even or, better yet, earns a profit on the maintenance work.

For retail businesses, create a special customer program.

You might create a special program where only club members get a discount on purchases. They might get advance notice of new products in the store, invitations to special events, or any other special things you can do in the store.

Follow these five steps to create your recurring revenue program:

1. Make a list of the products and services you will provide.
2. Make a list of the benefits of having these products and services.
3. Price the program where applicable.
4. Name your program.
5. Enroll your customers in your program.

These five steps answer the question, "What value does my recurring revenue program provide to my customers?"

Your name could be Frequent X program, X of the Month Club, Preferred Customer Program, or another name you create.

Maintenance programs may have a cost to provide the service. In these cases, calculate the cost of providing the service and price the maintenance program accordingly. The maintenance program may also provide a discount on other services, such as repairs, that a customer could need from time to time.

Once you have created your program, enroll your customers. Tell them the benefits of becoming a member of your program. Whenever a customer walks into your retail store, ask whether they would be interested in joining your preferred customer program.

Send out marketing messages about your program. Put a tab on your website with the benefits of your program and how to enroll.

If you have employees, get them involved in the program wherever possible. You might want to give them a small commission when they enroll a new member. You might have enrollment contests.

Have fun with it, grow the program, and build wealth.

Here are four principles to follow when you create your program:

- **Principle 1:** Recurring revenues should cover the overhead of your company. If the company's total overhead is covered, then you can breathe easier when slower times come. Many times it takes several years to accomplish this. Do it and you'll sleep better at night.

- **Principle 2:** For construction companies, have at least 1,000 recurring revenue customers for every $1 million in residential sales. Not there? Set a plan in place to have at least a minimum number of recurring revenue customers within a specific time frame.

- **Principle 3:** Be your own bank. If you want to decrease your dependence on a line of credit, get the discipline to deposit all of the recurring revenue monies you receive in an interest-bearing account. These funds accumulate quickly and can be your source when you are short of cash. Pay the interest to yourself rather than the bank!

- **Principle 4:** Set a contest with your employees to reach a recurring revenue goal. Make sure that everyone has bought into the need for recurring revenue. Then, start small with a three-month contest. Take a piece of poster board or put a chart on a white board (see Table 3). Along the X-axis should be the months. For example, March, April, May. Underneath each month should be two columns, one labeled "estimated" and one labeled "actual." Along the Y-axis should be everyone who is in contact with customers and has the opportunity to enroll recurring revenue customers.

Table 3. Sample Contest Diagram

	March		April		May		Total	
	Est.	Actual	Est.	Actual	Est.	Actual	Est.	Actual
John								
Jeff								
Jim								
Jane								
Totals								

Ask each person how many they think they can enroll during that three-month period. Put that estimate in the "estimated column" for each month. After you get everyone's estimates, total the estimated enrollments for the company. This is your three-month goal.

At the end of each month, record the actual numbers on the chart. At the end of the three-month period, determine the results. Did the company reach the goal or not? Is there a bonus or a penalty?

How to Account for Recurring Revenue

If your recurring revenue clients pay your company monthly and your company provides the services/products monthly, then revenue and cost are accounted for on your profit and loss statement.

If your recurring clients pay your company monthly or annually and your company provides the services/products at a different time than the monies are received, then your company has deferred income. This means that a customer has paid your company in advance for work not yet performed or services/products not yet provided.

In these cases, your company has a liability to perform. It has received money for work not performed or products/services yet to be received by your customer.

The monies that come in from the customer go in a savings account. The offsetting entry in your accounting package is deferred income—a current liability account on the company's balance sheet.

When the work is performed or products or services provided, the amount of the revenue for those products and services is transferred from the liability section of the balance sheet and put into the revenue section of your company's profit and loss statement.

Nothing has to be done with the savings account. The money can stay there unless your company needs it to provide the products and services. In this case, the savings is transferred into your company's operating bank account. Take the smallest amount that is needed. Savings will help build wealth.

Recurring revenue programs are the seeds that you plant to help your company have a great harvest for years to come.

Profit Rule 7: Understand That Profits and Cash Are Not the Same

Does this ever happen to you? You are confused about your profit and loss statement. The bottom line showed a profit month after month, yet you are having problems paying your bills. In busier months, the profit and loss statement shows a loss. This doesn't make sense to you.

And this year your CPA called you at tax time and told you that you owed the IRS a huge tax bill. Your profit and loss statement says your company was profitable, but where's the cash?

Here's the answer: Profits are just that: profits. It means that your revenues were greater than your expenses. A loss is when expenses are greater than revenue. Neither means that you have cash. Profits are a profit and loss statement item; cash is a balance sheet item. The two are very different.

Before I give a detailed explanation on how the cash comes into your business from a financial reporting perspective, make sure that your company is operating on an accrual basis rather than a cash basis as explained in the introduction of this book.

So, how does the company get cash from profits? Here is the detailed explanation: A revenue/sale (profit and loss statement) turns into an accounts receivable (balance sheet) when the company bills for the work performed. Then the company must collect for the work (balance sheet). If the company operates on a cash on delivery basis, accounts receivable instantly turns into cash (balance sheet). When the company gets its vendor invoices, they are entered as an expense (profit and loss statement), and this creates an accounts payable (balance sheet). Then the company pays its accounts payable (balance sheet), and hopefully there is cash left (balance sheet).

Some companies experience months when their company showed a loss, yet there is still cash in the bank. The opposite is also true: There are times where the company shows a profit and is having problems scraping enough cash together to pay payroll.

Warning: Even though the company's profit and loss statement shows a profit month after month, it can grow out of business. This happens when the company runs out of cash and doesn't have a line of credit or savings to cover temporary cash shortages.

Here are five ways profitable companies go broke:

1. Doing profitable work and collecting for it months later or never collecting for it...after the company paid employees and suppliers.

2. Not having timely, accurate financial statements so owners can make sure that projects/jobs are sold at a profitable price.

3. Using the cash method instead of the accrual method of accounting. The cash method of accounting almost always shows a profit, whether or not projects/jobs/widgets are profitable since companies generally don't

pay bills until they have cash to pay them. Or, in really busy months the profit and loss statement shows a loss because cash is plentiful to pay the invoices that have been piling up.

4. Performing profitable work and the client files bankruptcy during the middle of a project, leaving your company with hundreds of thousands of dollars in receivables that are uncollectable.

5. Purchasing too much inventory and having no inventory control. The company is betting its hard earned cash that it can sell what it has bought.

Here's a growth rule of thumb: A company needs 10% of its projected growth in cash to fund the growth. If the plan is to grow by $250,000 in a year, $25,000 in cash is needed to fund that growth. The cash is used for increased inventory, increased accounts receivable (if the company is not a cash on delivery company), increased overhead expenses, and potentially a vehicle or other fixed asset purchase.

Profits don't pay the bills. However, profitable jobs are necessary to pay the bills. Collect for profitable work quickly, pay the bills associated with that job, and stay solvent.

Profit Rule 8: Review Timely, Accurate Financial Statements Each Month

Financial statements are your scorecard. You must have them to properly price, make sure you are earning a profit, spot minor issues and resolve them before they become major crises, and make good business decisions.

Surprise! In the beginning, I will settle for inaccurate financial statements over no financial statements each month. This shows that the company owners are getting in the habit of receiving monthly financial statements. Once owners are in the habit of receiving them and asking good questions about them, they get more accurate.

A financial statement prepared by the company's accountant quarterly is unacceptable. Shoeboxes delivered to the company accountant at the end of the year are unacceptable. Timely, accurate financial statements prepared by the 15th of the following month (preferably by the 10th) give owners the ability to spot and fix minor problems before they become major crises.

The long-term survival of a business depends on them.

The first thing to do when receiving financial statements is to do a quick review (see Wealth Rule 1). If something looks wrong, question it and get it right before going any further.

Once the statements are as accurate as possible, calculate the 10 ratios that answer these operations questions:

- Can the company pay its bills?
- Is inventory too high? Is it increasing or decreasing?
- Is there a collections problem coming up?
- Is there a personnel productivity problem?
- Is there too much debt or is the level increasing?

These 10 ratios are divided into liquidity ratios, debt ratios, compensation ratios, and usage ratios. My book *The Courage to Be Profitable* gives a detailed description of how to calculate each ratio and how to interpret what the ratios mean. I will summarize each next.

The first group of ratios is the liquidity ratios. These ratios answer the question, "Is there enough cash coming in on a consistent basis to pay the bills?" The liquidity ratios are current ratio, acid test or quick ratio, and accounts receivable to accounts payable.

$$\text{Current Ratio} = \frac{\text{Current Assets}}{\text{Current Liabilities}}$$

$$\text{Acid Test} = \frac{\text{Current Assets} - \text{Inventory}}{\text{Current Liabilities}}$$

$$\text{AR/AP} = \frac{\text{Accounts Receivables (trade)}}{\text{Accounts Payable}}$$

The second group of ratios is the debt ratios. These ratios answer the question, "Is there too much debt or is the company getting deeper and deeper into debt?" The debt ratios are debt to equity and long-term debt to equity.

$$\text{Debt to Equity} = \frac{\text{Total Liabilities}}{\text{Total Equity}}$$

$$\text{Long-Term Debt to Equity} = \frac{\text{Long-Term Liabilities}}{\text{Total Equity}}$$

The third group is the productivity ratio. It answers the question, "For each dollar in revenue how much is the company spending on payroll and payroll taxes?"

$$\text{Productivity Ratio} = \frac{\text{Total payroll plus payroll taxes}}{\text{Sales}}$$

The fourth group is the usage ratios. These ratios answer the question, "Is the company building too much inventory or headed toward a collection problem?" The usage ratios are inventory turns and days and receivable turns and days.

$$\text{Receivable Turns} = \frac{\text{Annualized Sales}}{\text{Accounts Receivable (trade)}}$$

$$\text{Receivable Days} = \frac{365}{\text{Receivable Turns}}$$

$$\text{Inventory Turns} = \frac{\text{Annualized Material Expense}}{\text{Inventory}}$$

$$\text{Inventory Days} = \frac{365}{\text{Inventory Turns}}$$

Plot the ratios on a monthly and trailing basis (looking at a year's worth of data a month at a time). The monthly data and the trailing data are on two separate graphs. The trends are more important than monthly data. Here are five areas to watch out for:

1. If the company's current ratio and acid test are decreasing (current ratio and acid test lines are trending downward), most of the time the company is becoming less profitable. Even if the profit and loss statement shows a profit, the company is less profitable overall. Find out why.

2. If the inventory days line is increasing, the company is building up too much inventory. Even a five-day increase in inventory days is significant. That's an extra week's worth of inventory. Discover what is happening.

3. If the receivable days line is increasing, the company is headed toward a collection problem or has one. Like inventory days, a five-day increase is significant. It is taking a week longer to get paid. Why?

4. If the overhead is trending upward, then the company is spending more each month, as a rule, on overhead. Discover what is being spent and whether it is a reasonable expense.

Figure 1

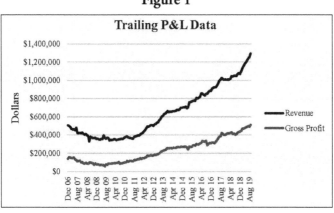

5. If the distance between the revenue line and the gross profit line on the trailing profit and loss data is increasing, as in Figure 1, the company is generating more revenue at lower gross margins. It might be better to have fewer sales at higher gross margins to ensure that the gross profit line is always higher than the overhead line (i.e., the company is profitable on a long-term basis).

Profit Rule 9: Understand That Inventory Is a Bet

Inventory is a bet. Companies who have inventory bet their hard-earned dollars that when they purchase a part, equipment, or other materials, the company can sell what has been bought. Look in the company trucks and in the warehouse to see if good or bad bets were made.

First, the company has to track inventory. I've seen it where the same value is on the balance sheet until the count at the end of the year. This is *not* a good way to track inventory.

Here is Philip's story:

Philip never tracked inventory throughout the year. He had the same inventory number every month until he counted it the following year. For years his count was within 1% of the amount on the balance sheet, so he never worried about it. Last year, when he counted it, there was a significant loss, about $10,000 less than the balance sheet said there was. This deduction went directly against his profits, so the company showed a loss after the inventory count rather than a profit. He was upset. Did the parts get lost, damaged, stolen, or just not billed to the customer? He didn't know and vowed to keep a better track of inventory the following year. He tracked purchases and wages on his profit and loss statement and balance sheet to make sure everything got invoiced to the customer and nothing was being stolen.

Track it and count it yearly. Spot check it monthly. Then, if the inventory doesn't match, dig deeper.

How much is too much inventory? Look in two places. First, look at the spread between current ratio and acid test lines. If the two lines are parallel, then the company is usually using inventory well. If the two lines are getting wider apart, then inventory is building up.

Second, if inventory days are increasing, this should be a warning sign that excess inventory could be purchased on a regular basis.

Here are seven procedures to put in place so that inventory becomes less of a bet:

1. Lock up the warehouse! Eliminate warehouse super-markets where field personnel can take whatever they want for a job or their truck. If materials are taken out of the stock room, what was taken is recorded (most simply) on a piece of paper and transferred to that employee's stock.

2. Barcode. Barcoding software has become inexpensive. Barcoding easily tracks what material comes in and out

of the warehouse and what material is used on jobs and service calls.

3. Use purchase orders for all materials. If the equipment/materials are ordered for a sold project/job, then these materials never hit inventory. They go directly to material expense. At the end of the month, make sure the inventory was received (packing slips should be attached to the purchase orders) and matched with the vendor invoices to ensure the company is paying the proper price for materials.

4. One person is responsible for all inventory. If multiple employees on equal levels (i.e., none of them report to each other) have access to inventory, then responsibility for accurate inventory is impossible.

5. If a field employee goes to the parts house for a part, the purchase order for that part is made part of the bill for that customer. If the materials are used from his truck, these materials can automatically be transferred out of inventory to material expense.

6. A material sheet for projects/jobs is required. Inventory can be pulled for each job and be ready for the employees to take it to the job. Or, for multiple-day jobs, it can be delivered to the job site.

7. Materials not used on the jobs are returned to the warehouse with a return material sheet.

Make sure your company places good inventory bets.

Profit Rule 10: You Can't Take a Percentage to the Bank

I hear company owners brag about their bottom-line percentage or their gross margin percentage. Neither of these percentages really matter. What matters is the bottom-line dollars or that the gross margins are consistent.

Bottom-Line Percentages

Those who talk about bottom-line percentages turn those percentages into dollars in their minds. What were the actual bottom-line dollars? That's what they really care about. They can't take the percentage to the bank. They can only take dollars to the bank.

Go one step further: What was the actual net profit per billable hour? This is the number that really matters. Net profit per hour comparisons are the most accurate company comparisons. When owner's compensation is added back to net profit, then net profit per hour comparisons truly define which company is most profitable.

Let's look at three companies:

Company	Revenue ($)	Net Profit ($)	Net Profit (%)	Billable Hours	Net Profit / Hour ($)
A	2,000,000	200,000	10	10,000	20
B	2,000,000	200,000	10	8,000	25
C	1,000,000	100,000	10	4,500	22.22

All three companies have the same net profit percentage. Company B is the most profitable. It has the highest net profit per hour. Company C with half the revenues as Company A, is more profitable than Company A. The percentage doesn't matter. The net profit dollars do.

Gross Margin Percentages

Comparisons of gross margins among companies are unreliable. Gross margin is defined as gross profit divided by sales. Gross profit is revenue minus direct expenses or cost of goods sold (i.e., an expense you incur because you sold something). Gross margins vary widely, depending on what expenses are put in direct cost and what expenses are put in overhead costs. There are three major variables: labor to produce the product/service, salesperson compensation, and truck expenses.

Labor expense is the greatest variable. Companies can include only the direct cost of labor to perform a job or provide service in cost of goods sold. Or they might put all labor expenses in cost of goods sold. This includes vacation, holidays, meeting time, and nonbillable time. The next choice is to break out all unbillable time (vacations, meetings, etc.) and put that time in overhead. The fourth choice is to include benefits in cost of goods sold, including FICA, Medicare, workers compensation, etc.

Most company owners do not include non-revenue-producing time or benefits in cost of goods sold. This makes it easier to track direct cost and overhead costs. Some divide overhead costs into overhead compensation costs and other overhead. All benefits and unbillable time go in overhead compensation costs.

Salesperson compensation is the second variable. If a salesperson is paid a salary plus commission, then the commission goes in cost of goods sold and the salary goes in overhead expenses.

Companies that put all of the costs listed above in cost of goods sold will have a lower gross margin than companies that only put hourly cost for direct labor and commissions in cost of goods sold. They will also have a lower overhead cost than companies that do not put all of the costs listed above in cost of goods sold.

The key is for gross margins to be consistent. If they are consistent, owners know that their pricing and the costs to produce those sales are consistent. They also know that the profit and loss statement is probably accurate, with all revenues matching expenses incurred producing those revenues in one month.

If gross margins are negative, that means that the company purchased goods/labor and sold it for less than it purchased them for. This isn't likely. Usually when this occurs, revenues are in one month and the expenses incurred producing those revenues are put in another month (i.e. financial statement fruit salad—see Profit Rule 4). It is imperative to match revenues and expenses so owners can make sure pricing is correct.

Percentages don't matter. Dollars do.

WEALTH RULES

|||||||||||||||||||||||||||||||||||||||||||||||||||||||||||||||||||||||||||||||

These 10 rules help you build your company's value—that is, wealth.

Wealth Rule 1: Pay Attention to Your Balance Sheet

Your balance sheet is where you build wealth. This financial document tells you true profitability. The longer you are profitable, the more opportunity you have to build wealth. This doesn't mean that you *will* build wealth. You must take the steps to actually build it.

Your balance sheet shows you how healthy your business is. It started the day that your company started or the day you bought it. It ends the day you close the doors or sell it.

Your balance sheet gives you warning signs. It tells you:

- If your profitability (i.e. long-term profits) is increasing.
- If you can pay your bills.

- If your debt levels are getting too high.
- If your inventory levels are getting too high.
- If you are heading toward a collection problem.

Your balance sheet must be accurate. Here are seven common balance sheet mistakes.

1. Negative Cash

You cannot have negative cash on your balance sheet. This means that there is a negative cash balance in your checking account. If this is the case, you are writing checks without money in the bank to cover them. If that is happening, your bank will quickly close your account and your company will incur huge insufficient funds charges.

Often when I see a negative cash balance, the company's bookkeeper has written the checks for all of the bills due in a month. They are sitting in the bookkeeper's drawer until enough cash comes in to pay those bills. At the end of the month, if enough cash has not come in to cover the bills, the balance sheet shows a negative cash balance. Even worse, it shows a smaller amount of accounts payable due. You think you owe less than you actually do.

Your accounting software does not care what the balance is in your checking account. It only cares that debits match credits (for example, the credit is the check amount and the debit is payment of the invoice). It doesn't send you a warning signal when your cash is negative.

Your bookkeeper should only write checks when there is cash to cover those checks. Otherwise, you are fooling yourself about the health of your business.

2. An Even Inventory Number—or No Inventory

For companies that have inventory, there is less than a one in 1 million chance that your inventory is exactly $20,000 or $3,500. Or the inventory value is the same every month. When I see this I know that inventory is not being properly tracked and that material cost is usually not accurate, either. Or, if I see no inventory on the balance sheets for companies that do have inventory, I know the statements are wrong.

Inventory is a bet (see Profit Rule 9). You've bet your hard-earned dollars that when you buy a part or piece of equipment that you can sell it at a later date. Make sure you make good bets.

3. A Balance Sheet That Doesn't Balance

The definition of a balance sheet is that assets equal—i.e., balance—liabilities plus net worth. If your balance sheet doesn't balance, then someone has incorrectly entered information to your computer system. You cannot make any good decisions about your business when the balance sheet doesn't balance.

There are times that the balance sheet doesn't balance in QuickBooks statements. QuickBooks gives you a warning and asks you if you want to rebalance the balance sheet. Do it. Balance sheets must balance.

4. Negative Loan Balances

A negative loan balance means that the bank owes your company money for a loan. The company owes the bank the loan amount; the bank doesn't owe the company. Generally, when I see this, it is close to the end of the loan payments. As the bookkeeper is making the monthly payments, the bookkeeper has entered the entire monthly loan payment as a decrease of the loan liability.

This is incorrect. Part of the monthly loan payment is principal reduction of the loan amount and part is interest the bank is charging your company for the privilege of having the loan. The interest is an expense to your business and is shown on your profit and loss statement. The loan principal reduction is shown on your company's balance sheet.

5. Negative Payroll Taxes Payable

Like negative loan balances, it is unlikely that the Internal Revenue Service or your state revenue department owes your company money. If so, the bookkeeper has made an error in the payment calculations.

Negative payroll taxes are normally an incorrect entry from payroll. Payroll deductions are normally in two pieces, and this is where the error is normally made. The first piece is a payroll deduction for income tax withholding, FICA, and Medicare taken from the employee's wages. The second piece is a matching FICA and Medicare charge that the company pays. This is an expense to the business and is shown on the profit and loss statement. Generally, negative payroll taxes happen when both the company and employee payroll taxes are entered incorrectly.

In addition, the federal government and most states have a labor unemployment tax, which is a small portion of payroll. This is an expense on the profit and loss statement and should not be a negative balance on the company's balance sheet.

6. Net Income on the Profit and Loss Statement Doesn't Match Retained Earnings

These two numbers must match. The net income from the profit and loss statement is transferred to the balance sheet. The amounts shown must exactly match! If they don't, then make sure that both the profit and loss statement and balance sheet show the same date (e.g., both are reported as of January 31, February 28, etc.). Then make sure both are shown on an accrual basis. If the year-to-date net profit and year's retained earnings aren't consistent, then someone is probably embezzling from your company.

7. Accounts Receivable and Accounts Payable on the Balance Sheet Don't Match the Accounts Receivable and Accounts Payable Balances Shown on the Aging Reports

Print out reports showing the list of accounts receivable and accounts payable each month when you receive the company's financial statements. These reports are called aging reports. They show how many receivables are current (under 30 days), how many are 31 to 60 days, etc. This is called an aging report. The total at the end of the accounts receivable and accounts payable should match the value printed on the balance sheet. If they don't match, someone has usually put entries in through journal entries rather than through your accounts receivable and accounts payable systems. Find out what those entries are and why they were made that way.

Checking for these seven errors takes less than 5 minutes. Correcting them may take longer.

Wealth Rule 2: Separate Business Expenses from Personal Expenses

What does this have to do with wealth? Building cash is critical for building wealth. Some small business owners use their business as a personal checkbook. They mix business expenses with personal expenses. In this case, it is very hard to tell whether their business is earning a profit or has a loss. Without profit, they cannot build wealth.

Sometimes business credit cards are used for personal expenses. The business pays for the credit card expenses, both business and personal.

Yet, you say, "It's my business and I can run it as I please." That is true. However, don't fool yourself when you review your financial statements every month. You cannot tell whether the business is earning a true profit when business and personal expenses are mixed.

Here is Zack and Anna's story:

Zack and Anna started and operate a business with 10 employees. The owners and several of the employees have company credit cards. There were no controls on the credit cards. The employees took the clues from the Zack and Anna's actions. When they got gas they also got food. When they went to pick up supplies, they also got a few things for themselves. Employees saw Zack and Anna regularly put their personal expenses on the business credit card, including travel, entertainment, PayPal purchases, Amazon purchases, and more. In addition, they paid their personal utility and other expenses for their children and their homes through the business. Employees felt they could do the same. They were taking clues from the owners.

Zack and Anna couldn't understand why the company wasn't earning as much profit as it should. They considered raising prices. Yet, they knew that wasn't the answer.

With my help, controls were put in place. The company credit card was taken away from a few employees. Credit card statements were scrutinized. Receipts became required. Payment of personal expenses through the business stopped. And yes, Zack and Anna gave themselves a raise so that they could personally pay for personal expenses.

What happened? For the first time, the owners could see if the company was profitable. Profitability actually increased because employees' and owners' expenses were not paid out of the business. At this point, the business could start building wealth knowing the profits were there.

The first step in separating business from personal expenses is having both a business and a personal checking account. This seems obvious to most business owners. However, there are many solopreneurs or startup business owners who have one checking account. It is impossible, as the company grows, to build wealth if all of the funds are commingled. To have a business, you need a business checking account.

Have separate business and personal credit cards. Even if all of the credit cards are in the owner's name, have some that are used strictly for business and others that are used strictly for personal expenses. Many owners go further when they issue credit cards to employees and have specific restrictions on, for example, gasoline credit cards, in terms of what can be charged to that card.

If you have been using your business for personal expenses, then give yourself a raise to cover the expenses that the business has been paying. Start thinking business wealth. And, if you want to build personal wealth, too, then when profitability is continuously good, consider taking cash out of the business to start building personal wealth.

Here is Mary's story:

Mary slowly built a recurring revenue program in her business. She religiously saved all of the money that was generated through this program in a special savings account. Her customer retention rate in the program was over 90% so she knew that this program was beneficial to her customers.

In addition, her employees believed in the program and enthusiastically told customers about it and the benefits they had personally received from the program services. No, the employees didn't have to pay for the program services. Mary used it as an employee benefit.

Within five years Mary had saved more than $250,000. She realized that it was the FDIC maximum insured amount that she could have in that bank. So, she moved it to another financial institution that was relatively safe (in her mind) in case she ever needed the money. This money would fund her retirement.

Here is Amy's story:

Amy also built a recurring revenue program for her company. In the savings account was over $500,000. It was time to purchase new trucks. She had the opportunity from her bank to finance the trucks at a 2% interest rate or use the funds from the recurring revenue savings account (all of the services had been delivered, so the funds were company funds—no current liability for that work existed).

She did the math, and even though the interest rate was low, she decided to use the recurring revenue cash to purchase the trucks since she was conservative and did not want any debt on her company's balance sheet.

Building cash gives you options when it comes to major purchases and retirement.

Wealth Rule 3: Build Recurring Revenue from a Wealth Perspective

Recurring revenue is critical from both a profit and a wealth perspective. The profit perspective is covered in Profit Rule 6.

Recurring revenue gives you a platform to build wealth. Your business will cease at some point. Hopefully you will sell it or pass it along to the next generation and reap the wealth rewards of your efforts over the years. Or it may cease abruptly upon your disablement or death. It is much better to plan for the exit than to have it happen when you are least prepared.

Brad Sugars, who started with nothing and became a billionaire, says, "Work once and get paid forever." This is how he built his wealth.

A business owner asked me to value his heating and air conditioning business. He had been working for more than 30 years and he was tired. He wanted to sell the business.

In the heating and air conditioning business, recurring revenue is generated with maintenance plans: taking care of heating and air conditioning equipment so that it lasts longer, owners pay lower utility bills, and more.

Unfortunately, the business had low profits and very few maintenance plans. The business was worth less than $100,000—not much value for 30 years of hard work. The owner was disheartened that his business was worth so little. It's what happened because he paid attention only to profit and not building wealth.

The wealth of your business is in customers who buy from your company year after year. Your recurring revenue customers provide a stable revenue stream for a purchaser. When your recurring revenue customers stay with your company year after year and they provide positive cash flow, the purchaser can be reasonably assured that he is investing in something that will also provide value and wealth to him as he operates the company.

The more recurring revenue your company has, the more wealth it has.

Wealth Rule 4: Build a Great Culture That Is Not Dependent on You

To build wealth, your business has to survive without you. Can you take a vacation without worrying about your business? Can you go to a conference, a trade show, or another business meeting for a few days without worrying about the business? Do you have a great management team who can run the business in your absence?

Can your employees run it without destroying it? Do your revenues stop when you stop working?

And even more important: Do you have to have control? This is probably the largest wealth destroyer. As your business grows, there will come a point when you cannot do everything yourself. If you try, you will be miserable and the business will suffer because things are slipping through the cracks.

I call these no-man's-land scenarios.

John built his company from the ground up. He started working out of his house and grew the business. It was operating in a 5,000 square foot building with eight employees. At that point, all the decisions were still made by him, even though he had a hard time getting everything done. Mistakes started to happen, and no one wanted to tell him about them because they knew he would blow up. In addition, his personal life was a mess. He didn't have time for his wife and kids since the business was consuming him.

John was in no-man's-land. He got help. Policies and procedures were put in place. He learned to let go and give a few of his employees the responsibility, accountability, and authority to make decisions. He made them managers. Not all of them survived as managers. He found others who could help grow the company. Now the company has 35 employees with a great team of managers. The company is not dependent on him. He has a better relationship with his wife and children. And, with the wealth that he built, he is planning to sell the business to the employees at some point.

Even if you are a solopreneur, you can have revenues not dependent on you. How? Automatic shipping of products monthly or quarterly, books, manuals, audio recordings, and other products that generate revenue and wealth for years to come. Tim Ferriss talks about the four-hour work week. He built a lifestyle business that was not dependent on him.

You can build a business with no employees or hundreds of employees. The choice is yours. If you choose to build a business with employees, you must build a great culture as it grows.

Building a great culture means building a team of people who can manage the business without you being there every minute. Once you have a great team in place, you can manage from afar, if you'd like, and do other things.

Building a great culture means people will be attracted to working in your business because they heard it was a great place to work. When this positive word of mouth spreads, you can find people even in an economy where the job market is tight.

If your company has a great reputation, then people will want to work there and want to stay there. You, as the owner, lead. You leave the management to others who are probably better at it than you are.

Most owners are not great managers. They are better visionaries, leading the charge, who should leave the day-to-day details to the management team. The leaders keep in touch using key performance, financial, sales, and operational indicators. When any indicator starts trending the wrong way, the responsible manager must fix the issue.

If the business is dependent on you, then it does not have as much value as a business that is led by you and can survive if you are not there.

The toughest transitions can be from parents to children. The parents build the business, and the children want to take it over. The parents don't want to let go. And many times the children feel privileged or are forced to take over a business they don't enjoy and don't want to be a part of. This is why most family businesses rarely make it to the third generation and beyond.

If you are going to sell the business, then it has to not be dependent on you. For example, if you are the top salesperson for the company, when you leave, sales will fall because your customers are buying from you rather than the company.

Build a great culture and a business that is not dependent on you. This will build your business and personal wealth.

Wealth Rule 5: Monitor Your Cash

Here are daily and weekly activities you can do to monitor your cash.

First, check your bank balance online every day.

Here is Janine's story:

Janine is the bookkeeper at a growing company. She checks the balances and activities for the business accounts every day. One day Janine noticed two tiny deposits, each less than $1. She thought that the owner had set up another online account and just forgot to tell her. She asked him whether he had set up any new online accounts. He said no. Janine thought the deposits were strange since no one at the company had requested new accounts. She never thought to call the bank.

The next day the owner got a phone call from the bank asking whether they had authorized a $50,000 withdrawal from their account. Obviously, the answer was no, and the bank shut down that account. That's why those two deposits were made. A hacker was trying to see whether the account was real.

Always pay attention to cash coming in and going out. Cash is the first part of building wealth. It takes less than five minutes each day to see what deposits have cleared and what withdrawals were made. Make sure you recognize all of them. If you don't, start investigating to find out what they are.

Weekly, create a cash flow report. A weekly cash flow report helps you track the cash coming in and going out of your business that week and estimates the needs for the following week. Your bookkeeper puts this statement on your desk every Friday afternoon along with a copy of the company's receivable and payable list. They should take no longer than 15 minutes to prepare, assuming that accounts receivable and accounts payable are up to date. The weekly cash flow report format is shown in Figure 2.

Figure 2

WEEKLY CASH REPORT

Week of _____ Prepared by _____

Cash on hand at the beginning of the week:

Petty cash	$ _____
Checking account 1	$ _____
Checking account 2	$ _____
Payroll account	$ _____
Money market	$ _____
Other savings	$ _____

Total beginning cash $

Cash collected	$ _____
Credit card payments collected	$ _____
Accounts receivable collected	$ _____
Other infusions (loans etc.)	$ _____

TOTAL AVAILABLE CASH FOR THE WEEK $ _____

Disbursements:

Payroll	$ _____
Accounts payable	$ _____
Loan payments	$ _____
Other	$ _____
Total disbursements	$ _____

ENDING CASH FOR WEEK $ _____

Estimated requirements for next week:

Accounts receivable to be collected	$ _____
Payroll	$ _____
Accounts payable to be paid	$ _____
Loan payments due	$ _____

TOTAL ESTIMATED CASH SURPLUS

(NEEDS) NEXT WEEK $ _____

Beginning cash is the cash you have at the start of the week: petty cash, cash in your operating checking accounts, payroll checking account, and money market funds. It is not stock investments or long-term investments. It's cash. It's what you're using to cover checks you've written.

Next, determine your cash receipts this week. You receive cash when your clients pay you for work performed—that is, when you collect on sales. Collections on sales come in many forms. You may receive cash, credit card payments, and checks. Each is tracked as a separate line item. Remember, cash is generated by its collections on sales, not sending the invoice to the customer.

Other inputs might include interest income or borrowing from the bank line of credit. There might be an investment in the business (e.g., an owner made a loan to the company or sold additional stock). There might be a sale of an asset where you received cash for that asset.

Total cash available is beginning cash plus all inputs are cash that the company receives this week.

Disbursements are cash going out of the company this week. Disbursements are the checks written for accounts payable, payroll, loan payments, purchases of inventory and other assets, and payment of overhead expenses.

Ending cash is total cash available minus disbursements. Ending cash must be positive. Without enough cash you need to decide which vendor isn't getting paid. Sometimes those are the tough decisions. Have the courage to make them.

Once you calculate ending cash for the week, estimate collections and disbursements for the upcoming week.

Estimate accounts receivable that are going to be collected, payables and loan payments that must be paid, and what payroll will be. Then take ending cash for this week, subtract payroll for next week and disbursements for next week, and add to it expected collections for next week. The end result should be a positive number. If it's not, time must be spent on collections or deciding which vendor isn't going to get paid.

The weekly cash flow report forces your company to be current (up to date with entries) for receivables and payables entries each week. This makes it easier to produce timely monthly financial statements each month.

As previously stated, your bookkeeper should put this statement on your desk each Friday afternoon. If that number is negative—that is, you need more cash next week—it's a lot easier to have a week to collect that cash rather than the bookkeeper knocking on your door on Thursday saying, "We don't have enough to make payroll," when payroll is due on Friday.

Wealth Rule 6: Save Cash

Building your cash balance is the first step in building wealth.

How much cash do you need? The answer depends on your tolerance for risk. Some owners choose to have three months of overhead expenses in the bank at all times. Others want six weeks of payroll. Others want a year's worth of operating expenses. Others have less than a month's operating expenses saved.

The choice is yours. It depends on how cyclical your business is and how easily you can contact your customers to generate additional revenue when needed (another reason why recurring revenue customers are so critical).

Some business owners live off their lines of credit and don't have much cash saved. What happens when the bank changes hands or the management philosophy changes and they call your line of credit—even it if is current?

Here's Steve's story:

Steve had a very profitable business with a line of credit exceeding $1 million. The business was cyclical and the perfect candidate for a line of credit. Each year before their busy season, they would use the line of credit. Then, when they were in their busy season, they would pay off the line of credit. This pattern went on for more than five years. The line of credit was current, and the company abided by the rules for using the line of credit (being zero for at least 30 days out of each year).

One day, during the start-up of their busy season, Steve got a call from his banker. The banker said they were calling the line of credit and he had 30 days to come up with more than $1 million. Steve was in shock. After all, the line was current, and they had had this line for many years. The banker said the bank was under new management, and they were changing all credit policies. Steve's line of credit was no longer wanted by the new owners.

Steve didn't have $1 million in cash. He scrambled to find another banker and vowed to save the cash so that he would never be in this situation again. The company would be its own line of credit.

How do you save cash?

Every business should save 1% of all cash that comes in the door in a separate savings account. As this account grows, you can decide what to do with the cash in savings. That means invest it, not spend it on personal things.

Assume that you receive a check for $1,000 for work performed. The 1% savings is only $10. You still have $990 in your operating account to handle expenses. The $10 might not seem like a lot of money. However, $10 for each $1,000 deposited can add up a lot of cash that you could need for operations or tax payments in the future. It's easier to sleep at night knowing that there is cash available for payroll if a receivable is late or a vendor will give you a discount for early payment.

Here is George's story:

George owned a business that continually saved a portion of revenues. The dollar amount in that account grew large, and George decided to take some of the cash to fund an expensive personal toy. When I found out that he had taken the money out of the account, my question was, "Why did you touch the money? That was for your retirement. Do you know how much you have to generate to put that back?" I was nice about it, but firm. George realized what he had done, and the company worked extremely hard to put the money back in the savings account. The next year, around the same time, I called George and asked whether he was taking money out this year. His comment: "No. I gave my stupid gene to my competitor!" George had learned a hard lesson.

The initial savings account should probably be in the bank where you have your operating account. This way you can transfer 1% of the deposit each week when your bookkeeper prepares the weekly cash flow report or each time you make a deposit. As the amount in that account grows over the maximum federally insured amount, consider moving some of it to an account that provides interest and is not in the same bank. This will decrease your temptation to take it out on the spur of the moment. You may also want to invest in some non-liquid wealth-building assets.

Here is Jack's story:

Jack was in the audience during a presentation where I talked about saving 1% of all revenues that come in the door. He raised his hand and asked if he could tell a story. I said yes. Jack said that he was in another one of my presentations in the mid 1990s, where I talked about saving 1% of revenues. He started doing it and built up a large sum of money. When the recession hit in the mid to late 2000s, the building next to his building came on the market at a very cheap price because the owner of that building needed money. Jack had the money in the savings account, so he wrote a check for the building next to his building. He rented the space and had positive cash flow on that building. He told the audience and me that he had recently sold the building for a lot of money. And Jack gave his thanks for me giving him the idea to save 1% of revenues.

Here is Charlie's story:

Charlie decided to save most of the revenues from his recurring revenue clients. Within a year he had saved more than $400,000. He started doing work that would normally require a line of credit from the bank because the customers were government customers who did not pay as quickly as other customers. He made the decision to use the $400,000 for his own line of credit and didn't have to hassle with a bank line of credit.

You might not be able to save all revenue from recurring revenue sales if a portion of that revenue must be used to produce the products and services for that recurring revenue customer. Save the rest.

The key to saving is to be consistent. Every bank deposit should have 1% of the deposit amount transferred to a savings account. Or, when your bookkeeper calculates your weekly cash flow report described in Wealth Rule 5, the transfer can be made once a week. Just do it on a regular basis.

Wealth Rule 7: Have a Sound Collection Policy

If you don't have the cash to make payroll, it doesn't matter what your sales are.

Many business owners are more concerned with making the sale rather than collecting the money for that sale. But if you don't collect on those sales, you can't pay your bills. Many business owners have gone through cash crunches because their customers went out of business while owing them a lot of money. Sometimes they didn't make it. Even though they had a profitable company, when their customers' businesses closed without paying them, they could not pay their bills and went under, too. You cannot pay payroll with profits. You must have cash.

So, what can you do to prevent this from happening? The critical thing is to watch your sales, collections, and payables each week. If you are like most business owners, you don't have a lot of time to deal with these issues. You don't have to deal directly with them; delegate the tasks and oversee the actions.

Restaurants, supermarkets, and retail stores are all cash on delivery. Can you imagine walking out of the grocery store without paying? If you are in business to consumer (B to C) sales, you *should* collect cash on delivery. Your customers expect it. This solves an accounts receivable problem.

For companies selling business to business (B to B) or business to government (B to G), accounts receivable are a way of life. Get a deposit when beginning the project. Make sure your company takes credit cards for payment and have clear payment terms. And, when that 30 days is up and you haven't received a check, then someone needs to make a phone call. Ask whether you can put the amount due on a credit card. Many times your customer will say yes. Then you have your money quickly.

Watch your cash each week. Your bookkeeper should print a weekly cash flow report for you to review each Friday (Wealth Rule 5). This report describes how much money you had in the bank at the beginning of the week, how much was added through collections on sales, and how much was subtracted through payment of bills. This gives you a cash balance at the end of the week.

The key to the cash flow report is the next part of the statement. It tells you how much money you can expect to come in the door the next week and what you expect to pay. If you don't have enough to cover all of your bills, then someone needs to start making telephone calls to people who owe you money. That person does not have to be you; it might be your bookkeeper. Just remember, unless you direct someone to make those telephone calls and follow up with you, those telephone calls won't get made.

It is important to do an accounts receivable and accounts payable aging each week to estimate the money coming in and the money going out. This way, on at least a weekly basis you are keeping track of where you are financially. It doesn't need to take up much of your time or your bookkeeper's time. Once the flow of information needed to complete these sheets is set up and running smoothly, it should only take 10 to 15 minutes each week to create this critical business management document.

Sales count. Profits count. But they are worthless if you don't collect the money those sales and profits generated.

A Note before Reading and Applying Wealth Rules 8–10

Wealth Rules 8–10 use trailing data. Trailing data produces the long-term trends for your company. It looks at a year's worth of numbers a month at a time.

For example, if you want to determine trailing revenue for January 2019, add the revenue from February 2018 through January 2019 and divide that result by 12.

If you want trailing to determine revenue for February 2019, add the revenue from March 2018 through February 2019 and divide that result by 12.

Looking at the January and February 2019 trailing data points gives you a trend. Is the graph increasing or decreasing? If it is increasing, then sales are increasing on a long-term basis.

Trailing data can be calculated for any metric you wish to track.

Wealth Rules 8–10 track trailing current ratio, inventory days, receivable days, and debt ratios.

The graphs show the trends of each metric and will be explained with the appropriate wealth rule.

Wealth Rule 8: Have a Sound Inventory Policy

Inventory is a bet. (Yes, I've said that before.) Inventory tracking is key to a sound cash policy. You don't want to spend cash you don't need to spend. The best ways to track inventory are to make sure it changes monthly on your balance sheet and monitor inventory days. If your company does not have inventory, then you do not calculate the ratios described below.

Inventory days are the number of days between the time a part is purchased to the time it is used to create a product or provide a service. Inventory turns are calculated on annualized costs. Calculate this ratio by using both the profit and loss statement and the balance sheet. It is calculated like this:

$$\frac{\text{Annualized Material Expense}}{\text{Inventory}}$$

or

$$\frac{\text{Annualized Cost of Goods Sold}}{\text{Inventory}}$$

The inventory days calculation is:

$$\frac{365}{\text{Turns}}$$

The inventory days ratio is calculated by using values from the balance sheet and the profit and loss statement. Most inventory days calculations use material expense only. Include total cost of goods sold when you have a business that has materials and labor linked to each other. For example, in the HVAC industry, when companies sell a part, they sell the labor to install the part. Anytime a company has material expense, it also has a labor expense. Thus, the ratio as I calculate it ensures profitable use of inventory by the field employees.

The inventory days are calculated from the inventory turns. The days trends are what you need to watch each month.

Figure 3 shows the trailing data points for these ratios.

Figure 3.

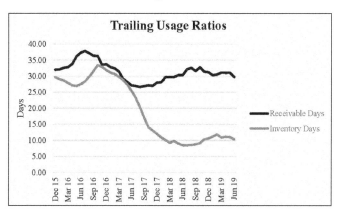

The trailing data graph for this client shows what happens when you don't pay attention to inventory. The company was not keeping track of inventory until the company got into a cash crunch. Then the owner tightened up the warehouse, hired a responsible inventory manager, and started tracking inventory. Inventory then decreased and remains stable now on a long-term basis, which means that the company is being efficient with inventory.

An increase of five days is significant because your company has an additional week of inventory. Find out why.

A sound inventory policy means tracking inventory days and making sure they are consistent.

Wealth Rule 9: Have a Sound Debt Policy

A good debt policy looks at your receivable days and your debt percentages.

First, receivable days are just that: How many days is it from the time you send an invoice to the customer to the time you get paid?

Your company's receivable days show whether the company is headed toward a collection problem. Figure 4 shows the trailing receivable days for a client. When the days start increasing collection calls get made and the receivable days decrease again.

Figure 4.

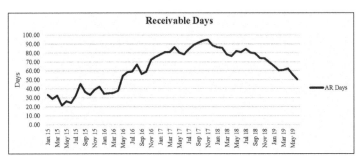

To calculate receivable days:

$$\text{Receivable Turns} = \frac{\text{Annualized sales}}{\text{Accounts receivable (+ cash)}}$$

$$\text{Receivable days} = \frac{365}{\text{Turns}}$$

If at least 50% of your company's sales are cash on delivery, add customer accounts receivable plus cash. Do not include accounts receivable from employees or owners.

Now let's look at debt ratios, the second part of a good debt policy.

There are two measures of debt (i.e., is your company starting to increase debt, or is it too debt-ridden?): the debt to equity ratio and the long-term debt to equity ratio.

The debt to equity ratio looks at all debt: current and long-term liabilities. The long-term debt to equity ratio looks only at long-term debt: those liabilities the companies owes for more than one year. These ratios are computed from your balance sheet each month.

To calculate these ratios:

$$\text{D/E} = \frac{\text{Total Liabilities}}{\text{Total Equity (i.e. net worth)}}$$

$$\text{LTD/E} = \frac{\text{Total Long-Term Liabilities}}{\text{Total Equity}}$$

Increasing debt to equity ratios mean that your company is becoming more debt-ridden. The most critical ratio is the long-term debt to equity ratio. For many businesses, it should be between zero and one. Any value over one means that the company has taken on too much debt and it is a burden to the company.

The debt to equity ratio doesn't have "an average value." I've seen this ratio as high as 11—and the company was still profitable. Most of the time when the debt to equity ratio increases dramatically, several large, long-term projects are in their initial stages. The company is purchasing significant quantities of equipment and materials. When this happens, you'll also see a high jump in accounts receivable, as the company bills for these materials.

Figure 5 shows the monthly graph of the debt ratios. It's hard to see what is happening because there are months when the debt to equity ratio is high and months when it is low. The long-term debt to equity ratio is staying fairly constant.

Figure 5.

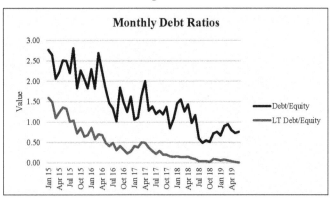

Figure 6 shows the trailing data or the trend of the debt ratios. Each point takes one year's data and divides it by 12.

Figure 6.

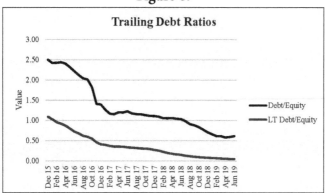

The company initially had a lot of short-term and long-term debt. Now all ratios are decreasing, and the long-term debt is almost negligible.

If you find that your receivable days are increasing, it's time to make collection calls. If you find that the company's debt ratios are increasing, find out what is being spent and whether those expenses are necessary.

Wealth Rule 10: Have an Increasing Current Ratio

An increasing current ratio generally means increasing profitability. A decreasing current ratio generally means decreasing profitability. The only times this is not generally a measure of profitability is when your company has large cash withdrawals for tax payments or asset purchases such as vehicles. In the case of vehicle purchases, the company is trading short-term assets (e.g., cash) for long-term assets (e.g., a vehicle). Current liabilities remain constant, so the current ratio decreases. This decrease is not due to less profitability. It happened because of an asset purchase.

Current ratio is calculated this way:

$$\frac{\text{Current assets}}{\text{Current liabilities}}$$

Figure 7 shows the graph of the data. The trailing graph shows the seasonality of the company: Profits increase in busy times and decrease in slower times. However, the overall trend is upward—that is, more profitable.

Figure 7.

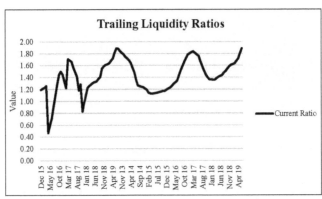

On a monthly review of the financial statements you can't tell that the company is losing profitability. Only when you look at the current ratios on a long-term trend can you see that the company must become more profitable each month to survive for the long term.

Here is Carl and Connie's story:

Carl and Connie grew their business to more than $3 million in revenues by only looking at sales numbers and cash. When it got to the point they could no longer manage the business without managers and financials, they begrudgingly got managers, and I helped them straighten out the financial side of their company. However, they never paid attention to them. There were always more pressing needs. After begging for financial statements for five months, I finally received them at the end of May. Table 4 is the current ratios for the five months that I got all at one time.

Table 4

	Dec 18	Jan 19	Feb 19	Mar 19	Apr 19
Current Ratio	1.05	0.98	0.87	0.85	0.80

The current ratio was under one and going down significantly each month. They were in financial trouble and didn't know it until it was too late to do much about it. Had the current ratio been monitored in January or, at the latest, February, actions could have been taken to reverse the downward trend. Now a cash crisis existed when it could have been prevented.

Get your financial statements every month and calculate your current ratio every month. Your company's current ratio should be monitored monthly. It should always be greater than one. It should be constant or trending upward. The only times downward current ratios are acceptable is if the company paid a huge tax bill or purchased assets using cash rather than a loan. In these cases, cash decreases and current liabilities remain the same, causing the current ratio to decrease. An increasing current ratio means increasing wealth.

Implementing the
Profit and Wealth Rules

|||||||||||||||||||||||||||||||||||||||||||||||||||||||||||||||||||||||||||||||

The five following avatars represent five typical business situations. Their stories should give you ideas about how to apply the rules of profit and wealth.

Zoe is two years out of college in a job she hates. She stays trapped because she has a mountain of college loans that she has to repay. She sees no way out until she decides to start a business on the side to help pay off the college debt. Then maybe she could get a job that she likes.

Ted has been in the janitorial business for three years. The business is growing and consuming him. He has no time for his wife and kids and feels guilty about it. His cash flow is always tight, which brings an additional strain on family life.

Leo is working for the family jewelry business. His grandfather and his dad have both promised him that he will own the business one day. So, Leo works really hard, believing the promise that he will reap the rewards at the end. The business starts struggling after his grandfather passes away, and his dad won't implement any of his ideas. After all, the way it has worked for the past 35 years should work now. They will get through it. With the business struggling, will there be any rewards at the end?

Samantha is a stay-at-home mom. She was a superstar salesperson who, for the last six years of her working career before she became a full-time mother, won all of the sales awards at the company she was working for. Then her husband and she decided to start a family and she became a stay-at-home mom. She was going crazy at home and decided to start a sales consulting business. After all, her thought was, "If I could sell, I could teach others to sell."

Julie and John bought a small heating and air conditioning business. Their goal has always been to grow it to $10 million in revenue. They have grown the business to about $4 million in revenue and have hit a wall for the past several years. It's frustrating, and they want to break through this wall.

Zoe's Story

I graduated from ABC University with a degree in communications. I took out student loans to fund my education. I got a job that I initially liked, but in the past two years I have grown to hate it. I count the hours until I can go home. The only reason I am still there is that I have to pay back $74,000 in student loans.

The loans are a mountain to me. It's a huge number that I'm not sure I will ever get out of. Every month I write a check, and it seems as if the balance never gets lower. And I'm stuck in this job because I have to be here to pay my monthly loan payments. I don't want to lose my job, and I can't afford to leave my job. I've looked around and can't find another job that I think I might be interested in. How am I ever going to afford a house or the other things I really want?

Maybe I should look for something to do in the evenings and on weekends that will give me some extra money. After all, the company I work for only gets 40 hours per week of my time. Maybe some of this other time can be used for something I enjoy and to give me some relief from the mountain of debt, give me a few bucks so I can go out to dinner more often and have a little fun.

I searched for jobs that I could do on the side. A friend started pet sitting and walking dogs. I grew up with two dogs and a cat. I've always loved animals, even though I can't have one of my own right now. I long for the day when a tail-wagging dog greets me at the front door when I come home from a bad day at work.

But I live in an apartment. No pets allowed. This won't work unless I go to people's houses and care for their pets there. A dead end, I thought.

But the idea of working with pets really intrigued me. How could I combine what I learned in college with my love of pets?

What about marketing for a dog walker like my friend who needs to get the word out? The problem is my friend doesn't have any money for marketing. She did this pet thing so she could make a little on the side…just like I am looking for.

Maybe I could find a vet who needed marketing and social media done for them? This is a possibility. I can do it on the side cheaply, a lot less than those big companies charge.

What about volunteering with the local nonprofit animal shelter to get some real-life experience doing social media and marketing? No money there. But it would be exposure and potential work from people who need marketing. And I love working with animals.

I get started. I am excited about something for the first time in a long time.

In the evenings after work, I spend hours researching and putting together a list of communications services that I can provide for veterinarians and the animal shelter. It's been a blast putting it together. I finally get to use my degree!

In the middle of all of the research, I found information on writing a business plan. Why should I write a detailed 35-page plan? This doesn't make sense to me. I look for something that isn't that big and detailed. After all, this is only a side gig. I found a three-page business plan format (see *The Courage to Be Profitable* for details)—a page for goals, a page for my marketing plan (which should be a piece of cake for me since I was a communications major in college), and a page for the budget. Budget, yuck! I hate numbers. But I'm going to stick with it because it will help me discover what my costs are and whether I am really making a profit. I need the money from this side business to help me get rid of the mountain of debt. Three pages shouldn't be that difficult.

My monthly student debt loan payments are $635 per month. I want to get enough money to pay these monthly loan payments and a little more so I can pay this mountain of debt off early.

I decided on one goal: Get rid of the loan debt. Clear at least $635 per month. This will help increase my wealth by decreasing my debt. Once it is paid off, I can start investing it in something that I really want.

I decided to focus on the financial side and put together a budget. There are very few expenses other than my time. I'm operating the business out of my home, and I don't have to buy materials. I just need to bill for my time. I decided that I am not going to consider a part of the rent or the utility bill as an expense right now. I might have a meeting to go to or office supplies to purchase each month. That would be at most $100 per month. So the income to me needs to be $735 per month.

The real question is how many hours per month can I bill? Assuming that I can bill 10 hours per month, which is only 2.5 hours per week, my net profit only needs to be $73.50 per hour to achieve my goal.

So, I decide to charge $75 per hour. This covers my needed $73.50 per hour plus a little more for me.

Now, how do I do this? What social media and marketing services can I provide that will pay me at least $75 per hour?

And who will pay me $75 per hour?

Wake up, Zoe! It's not the $75 per hour for me. What value can I provide to a vet that is more than $75 an hour or $750 per month so it's a no-brainer for them?

Can I get the vet more clients? Sales on some of their products? Marketing a recurring revenue maintenance plan for pets? This will help the vet generate more wealth for their business. Perhaps I can explain to them why this is important.

And, maybe I can charge $15 per new customer plan. This would be a way to build their wealth and mine. Wait, that means I have to help generate 49 new maintenance plans per month so that I get my $735 per month. This might be another way to promote the services.

Now that I have what I am going to do, I have to find a veterinarian who needs the social media and marketing help. I decide to volunteer at the animal shelter. This gives me real-world experience and proof that my social media and marketing services produce results. In addition, I will meet veterinarians and talk with them.

Over the next six months my boring job becomes less boring, and I am doing better there, too. Perhaps it is because I have something else that excites me. I actually got a raise! I decided to put the extra money into a savings account.

My social media and marketing work for the shelter has helped it raise more funds and get more people adopting these animals. I am loving how I am helping.

I also got to know three veterinarians. Two have become clients. I am building a recurring revenue program for both. And once these two are successful, then I can probably approach other veterinarians with the same idea.

It took six months to get the first veterinarian to say yes. As the work I did for him built his business, another one noticed and was interested in having me help him, too. Both are using the recurring revenue plan I created for the first veterinarian.

It took about a year to start generating $750 per month. Then, in the second year I got another veterinarian client and I am now seeing over $1,000 per month in my business bank account. I am using the funds to pay myself and to pay down my student loan debt.

The $15 per maintenance client was also easy for the veterinarians. They just added my $15 to the price of the agreement. Those funds, as I receive them, go directly to paying down debt in addition to the monthly required payments.

If I continue to get new veterinarian clients, I will have my student loan paid off in five years or less.

Ted's Story

I needed a job. My wife was pregnant with our first child, and I needed to earn money. I saw an ad for a cleaning service that was looking for people. I didn't have a lot of skills, and I knew I could clean. I applied for the job and became an employee.

At first it was great. I learned how to really clean. It was a lot different than I expected. But within two years I became frustrated.

One day I happened to see an invoice for one of our customers. I got so mad. The boss was charging the customer $300 per cleaning visit, and I was only making $30 per visit. I could do his job, charge the customer $280 a month, and make a killing. I was tired of working for a boss I hated, and this discovery made me want to start my business even more.

I talked it over with my wife, and we decided that I should start my own business. Even though I was only making a small hourly wage, we had a little savings. Our first child was doing well, and my wife's mother was taking care of him during the day so she could work, too. This would give us some money coming in even if the business didn't do well in the beginning.

So, I quit. It was scary at first. I had to do things that I never knew my former boss did. Find a customer? Bill the customers? Collect? Make sure everyone does their job properly? Do the bookkeeping? All I knew how to do was clean.

It's three years later, and I am exhausted. I'm working all the time, and I never see my children (we had a second child after I started my business). I can't seem to get ahead, and the profits are meager. If I ever want to spend time with my wife and kids, go on vacations, and experience the joys and freedom that my business is supposed to give me, something *has* to change.

I discovered the rules of profit and wealth. The first thing I did was realize that I was working 80 hours a week—and almost none of those hours were working on the business. I had two employees I had to oversee constantly to make sure they were taking care of our customers.

On top of that, I kept losing jobs to price. It seems that everyone thought that the janitorial business was easy to get into. They did what I did: Lower the price to get the work. And they did, in many cases. Of course, when our customers found out that they weren't getting the quality service that I provided, many came back. However, it was constant pricing pressure.

I decided to determine my overhead cost per hour. I looked at last year's profit and loss statement, which I really didn't understand well, and there were 6,000 billable hours, including my hours. The total overhead last year was \$200,000, so our overhead cost per hour was \$33.33.

Then I got really curious to see what my net profit per hour was last year. We earned \$22,000 according to the profit and loss statement. Where was it? I discovered that profits were not cash (Profit Rule 7) and that most of those profits were tied up in accounts receivable that I hadn't collected. Perhaps I should start taking credit cards and charge the cards monthly.

My net profit per hour was \$3.67. That was the biggest surprise to me. Why should I put myself through all this pain and stress for a measly \$3.67 an hour?

I talked to my wife about it. She was as surprised as I was about how little the company was actually earning. After we talked, we decided that I would stick with the business and figure out a way to generate more profit. She was not thrilled with her job but was willing to wait it out until I was making enough money so that she could stay home with the kids.

That, more than anything, was motivation to me to get going and plan out what to do: to give my wife something that she really wanted.

I decided that for this year, the minimum net profit per hour I would accept is \$10 per hour. That is three times what I earned last year and would be a good start.

Then I had to overcome this pricing pressure. I remembered Profit Rule 6 and Wealth Rule 3, which talked about building recurring revenue, a loyal customer base. How was I going to do that?

I decided to get into a niche: high-end customers who would be willing to pay higher prices because they wanted reliability and quality. They didn't want to come into their stores, offices, and restaurants and see a lousy cleaning job. I would give them an incentive, a maintenance plan, where they could invest a certain amount per month for a minimum of two years. I'd work hard to ensure they became loyal customers so that when a "cheaper price" company came calling, their response would be, "We are *so* happy with our current company that we are not interested in changing."

I found a niche: high-end restaurants that were persnickety about everything from the food to the appearance of the restaurant. They would pay higher prices for quality. They understood quality vs. low price, since that is how they approached their customers.

So, I began to price.

When I examined my hard cleaning costs, they were about $5 per cleaning. I charged extra for restocking toilet paper, paper towels, and soap if the customer did not want to supply them.

I decided to include these restocking costs for my recurring revenue customers as an advantage to join the program.

I calculated my prices as follows.

Net profit per hour: $10.

Overhead cost per hour: $33.33.

Minimum gross profit per hour: $43.

High-end restaurants wanted cleaning six nights per week. There were two people per restaurant, and the job normally took two hours, including travel time to the restaurant. So, four billable hours per night.

The total gross profit was $43 × 4 = $176.

I decided to pay my help more than anyone in the area as part of the pricing calculation. I decided to pay employees $20 per hour.

Total price to the customer for a cleaning that took two hours for two people:

Direct labor: $80 ($20 × 4 hours).

Direct cost: $5.

Gross profit: $176.

Price to the customer: $261 per night.

I decided to add one more step and include a preferred customer plan. In the preferred customer plan, the customer received a 15% discount on cleaning services as well as bathroom supplies included as part of the cleaning.

This would mean that the preferred cleaning price was $261 and the regular cleaning price was $312 ($261 / 85% + $5 for supplies).

Since I was charging more, I could pay my help more. They were now making more than all other cleaning services in the area. All of a sudden I had my pick of employees. I could make sure that they did what they were supposed to because there were others waiting to take their place.

The preferred maintenance plan gave me an edge. I could predict my revenue and my expenses each month.

Getting the first restaurant was the toughest. However, as I became better at selling, and as the restaurant owners realized they had one less headache, I started getting referrals from other restaurant owners. I also asked for referrals. Within a year I was doing the cleaning for most of the high-end restaurants in the area.

As a result of this success, I decided to find a person to take my place in the cleanings each evening. Now all I had to do was check the jobs, which took a lot less time. I also had more time to spend on the business, learning the other rules of profit and wealth.

Each year I recalculate my net profit per hour and overhead cost per hour. As the number of employees has grown, the overhead cost per hour per employee has dropped. This has enabled me to keep my prices consistent while increasing my net profit per hour.

And yes, within two years my wife was able to quit her job and stay at home with our children. I have more time to spend with them, and I am not as stressed out.

Even more important, I have a plan to increase the number of preferred customers, which builds my wealth.

Leo's Story

I am the third generation working in my family's jewelry business. My grandfather started it about 50 years ago in a store located in the main business area of our town. I grew up helping my grandfather and then my father in the store.

When my grandfather passed away, my father took over running the store. My father and my grandfather before him have always promised me that the store would be mine one day. I believed them and put my heart and soul into learning as much as I could about the jewelry business.

Our designers create unique pieces of jewelry that our customers are proud to wear. We often get new customers simply because they wanted to know where a friend got that necklace.

Times have changed. In the old days my grandfather could put an ad in the local newspaper and people would flock to the store. Then he got a scare because Walmart came to town. Many of the stores in downtown closed because they couldn't compete. Our company's jewelry was different and we remained open. Unfortunately, there are many unoccupied buildings downtown and fewer and fewer people are coming into the store.

My father refuses to let me do anything. He knows that the revenues are down but thinks that doing things the same way that his father did will solve the problem. He won't look at financial statements. He only knows that fewer people are coming in the store and he is having a harder time paying payroll.

I created real financial statements for the first time. I know my grandfather didn't do them. He operated only on cash. If there was cash in the bank, then the company was doing OK. My father did the same thing. He never looked at a profit and loss statement or a balance sheet. It was time to bring the jewelry store into the 21st century. I knew that I wouldn't get it here without a fight.

The first thing I did was calculate our overhead cost per hour and our net profit per hour. Our net profit per hour was less than I could earn at the fast food store down the street. Dad didn't want to pay attention and ignored me.

Then I calculated our balance sheet ratios. Our current ratio was going down each month. I learned that this meant that our profitability was decreasing month after month. Our debt ratios were increasing. Both of these ratios were going the wrong way.

We didn't have a receivables problem because people paid for their purchases when they made them.

Still, Dad kept his head in the sand and ignored me. I love this business, and I didn't want to see it fail. I wanted to keep the store in the family and pass it along to my children.

I knew that the only way that we were going to get customers back in the store or buying from us again was doing something different than we were doing. Dad still wanted to put the ads in the newspaper. I tracked the results and showed him that sales from those ads weren't even covering the cost of the ads. We didn't even have a decent website. Grandfather didn't do that, so Dad didn't do that, either. His thinking was, "We didn't need it in the past; why do we need it now?"

It was time for radical change.

It was time to rebuild the profits so we could rebuild the wealth.

It was time to create a preferred customer program.

I decided to go where people with disposable income went. If we couldn't get people to come into the store, it was time to go where they went. I remembered a story about a jeweler setting up a booth at a location where people bought horses. I remember thinking, "Why would you do that?"

When a man buys a horse, the conversation at home confessing that he bought a horse would be a lot easier if the man bought a horse *and* a gorgeous piece of jewelry for his wife.

Convincing Dad to spend the money for our first booth was not easy. He said no time and time again. I finally told him that I would use my money to do this. I wanted to make a point. When I went to that first horse sale, the revenues that day were higher than a month's revenues from the store. After this first success, Dad begrudgingly went along and allowed me to spend the company's money for the next booth.

Yes, revenues from that day were great. I realized that the most important thing about that day was that I asked for and got the contact information from almost everyone who purchased a piece of jewelry and even many who stopped by but didn't purchase anything. I had their permission to contact them again. My preferred customer program was beginning.

Then I created reasons to come to the store.

- We had "meet the designer" nights.
- We encouraged people to bring their jewelry that needed a facelift into the store. They liked the stones but didn't like the settings anymore. We created new settings for them.
- We encouraged people who inherited jewelry that they didn't like or want to bring it into the store. We purchased many pieces on consignment and promoted heirloom jewelry nights. These were wildly successful because these pieces were one of a kind, and when they were sold, there was not another one.

Over the next months and years, I tracked our financial ratios and preferred customer program. Every month the current ratio increased a little bit. Each month we added new customers to our preferred customer program. The profits and wealth increased slowly. We reversed the downward spiral and began the climb back to profitability and wealth. After about two years, the store was finally at a point where I was comfortable. I continue to track these metrics each month to make sure the jewelry store continues to head in the right direction.

And, by the way, Dad finally let me take over the running of the store once these activities increased the revenues and profits.

Samantha's Story

I was the top salesperson for ABC Company for six years. I won every award and always was invited to the trips given to the top salespeople. I enjoyed helping my customers, and I enjoyed the recognition.

My husband and I decided to have a family. I left ABC Company. In the beginning I loved it. It was something new, and I loved taking care of my two children. Don't get me wrong—I still love taking care of my children. Watching them grow and guiding them along the way gives me great pleasure.

But I wanted more. I wanted adult conversations. I wanted the recognition and rewards I got when I was selling. What could I do that would give me the adult conversations and recognition I craved while still having the time to take care of my kids?

One day, as I was walking with the kids, I got the brilliant idea to create a sales training company. After all, I knew how to sell. I had been through many training programs during the years I worked for my former company. What could be so hard about that?

I had many questions running through my mind:

- How long would the class be?
- How much would I charge for a class?
- Would there be follow-up after class? If so, what would it be and how much would it cost?
- What would the expenses be for the class?
- How much would it cost to promote the class?
- What was my time worth to me?

The toughest thing for me was pricing. Once I had the answers to these questions, I would know what the class would be and what the expenses for class would be.

My overhead cost per hour was minimal. Even though I would operate the company out of my home, I decided to use the current IRS regulations for home-based businesses to determine what the "rent" and utility costs would be. I estimated these yearly costs along with the number of billable training hours I would have.

Including the cost for a business checking account, business cell phone, and some office supplies, my overhead cost per hour was $5 per hour. I could live with that.

The big question was, "What net profit per hour do I want to earn?" To me it was a question of what my time is worth. I decided that my time was worth $300 per hour. After all, that is what my accountant and lawyer charge. I'm at least as good as they are. So, the minimum gross profit per hour was $305.

I decided that I would model my sales training classes on many that I had taken. Most were two days. That meant 16 hours in class. I estimated an additional 32 hours for class preparation, which meant a total of 48 hours.

I estimated the materials cost for 10 participants, room rental, and food for class to be an additional $2,000. The minimum I would need for each class was 48 × $305 + $2,000 = $16,640.

This meant the fee per class participant needed to be $1,664.

I could sell this. It was about what any former company paid for me to go to classes.

I contacted my former boss and explained that I was starting a sales training company. He said that he would be my first client. I knew that the company had spent a lot of money sending me to sales training classes. When I told him that the investment per salesperson was $1,664, he complained about the price. Ah, the typical sales objection I've heard a million times. I think he was testing me since I knew he had paid that much and more to send me to class.

I asked him whether he thought that as a result of sales training, each sales rep could increase their sales by at least $16,000. He said yes. Then the investment was worth it.

We set a date for my first class, and I sent him an invoice for $4,160, the deposit for the class. I estimated this 25% deposit was enough to pay for the room and training materials.

I now had to secure the location for class and create the materials for class. Securing the location was easy. I had a friend who had done classes in a training center, so I called them and reserved two days.

I created the materials for class during the times my children were napping and late in the evenings after they went to bed. I did my best work at night, so I spent at least three nights a week working on the class.

I tracked my hours and saw that it took much more than 32 hours to get ready for class, but I rationalized it because the prep time for the subsequent classes should be a lot less.

The first class didn't go as well as I had hoped. I realized that selling and teaching sales were two totally different skill sets. Even though it didn't go as well as I thought it should, everyone got sales training ideas, techniques, and processes from the two days. They also wanted to know how I had been so successful in the past.

In addition, I had to get someone to watch my children for the two days I was in class. They missed me, because this was the first time I had been away from them for two days. I explained that I didn't leave them and that I would be there in the evenings to find out about their day. My husband was thrilled that I was doing something that excited me again. We agreed that I would do no more than two training sessions per month.

I sent the final invoice to the company and was paid in 30 days. It was thrilling to get that additional $12,480 in my checking account.

As in my former sales days, I followed up with my former boss. The class participants were selling much more than the cost of class, and he was pleased. He wanted to set up another training class for other salespeople who didn't attend the first class.

I set up another date. In addition, I went through my list of contacts and found other potential companies that could send people to classes. I kept to the two classes per month per the agreement with my husband and increased our wealth at the same time.

Julie and John's Story

We bought a small heating and air conditioning company about 15 years ago. When we took over, there were two field people and the previous owner. His wife handled all of the office functions. She left when he sold the business to us.

In the beginning it was John in the field selling and working side by side with the two field people keeping customer's homes and offices comfortable. I was in the office answering the telephone, dispatching, and doing the books. For whatever reason, we always wanted a $10 million company. In the beginning we had no idea what that really meant. The $10 million number just sounded good.

Over the years the company grew. The two field employees became 20 field employees. John continued selling. The office also grew. Now there are dispatchers, a receptionist, and a bookkeeper. I oversee everything. John and I are still the only ones who sign checks and go to the bank every day.

We also review our financial statements every month and have since day one. In the beginning it was difficult to understand what they were saying. It became easier and easier as the months went by. Now we think we make great business decisions on accurate data each month. We know our overhead cost per hour and our net profit per hour and price accordingly. In slower times of the year, we lower our net profit per hour to keep the field busy. We never knowingly go below $25 net profit per hour. Most of the time, we price at $100 net profit per hour or higher.

Over the years we have been able to spot some issues that we took care of before they became major crises. One of the things we found was that one of our crews was not as productive as the other crews. We tried training, and that didn't work. We split them up and put them with other field personnel. This worked for one of the original crew members. The other went through a "career readjustment program" and left the company.

We also found overhead creeping up and delved into why. The problem was too much overtime for office personnel and no controls on what was purchased. We stopped that before it became a problem.

We were smart and built our maintenance base as we grew. Maintenance customers receive a heating maintenance and a cooling maintenance each year. We didn't believe in "kick the tires" maintenance, so our maintenance program was more comprehensive than many of our competitors' programs. We also were in contact with our maintenance customers at least once per month. We let them know how valuable they were and the benefits to remaining a maintenance customer. As a result, our renewal rates were over 90%. We were definitely building wealth and profit.

Now we are approaching $4 million in revenue and are finding it really hard to grow. We've been at this revenue mark for about three years.

John and I are tired. We find that we can't do everything ourselves, and things are slipping through the cracks. John is trying to manage service, sales, and installation. He is having a hard time keeping up and is getting frustrated.

I discovered that our company is in what's known as no-man's-land. We are at a point where, as we found out, we have to have policies and procedures in place that have to be followed. We can't run by the seat of our pants any longer. We also have to hire real managers. These managers manage each of the departments and are responsible for the bottom-line profitability of that department.

I also discovered that until we are through this stage our profits will decrease because we have to add the management layer of overhead—not a pleasant thought. However, if we are to grow to $10 million, then we have to get through this frustrating stage of business.

So, we invested in a procedures manual so that we didn't have to write it ourselves. That saved a lot of time with very little outlay of dollars. Now we just have to implement it and find good managers.

John initially thought that a few of the field people could make good managers. One of the service technicians thought he could be a service manager. He was the best technician that we had. I had heard too many stories about service technicians failing miserably at management. The skills needed to be a great service technician are not the skills needed to be a great service manager. When we explained the role of the service manager, he decided that he didn't want to deal with upset customers or technicians not doing their jobs. We created a field supervisory position for him where he could use his technical skills to help the other technicians.

Our office manager came to us and wanted the service manager position. We gave her a chance and were pleasantly surprised that she did an excellent job with the technicians and the customers. She quickly learned the department's profit and loss statement and how she could ensure the service department operated profitably.

We looked outside the company for an installation manager. The first installation manager came from another heating and air conditioning company. He didn't make it. We kept looking and finally found a manager from outside our industry who understand how to manage people and things. So far the installation department is running profitably.

John decided to keep the sales manager role himself. There were two salespeople he was mentoring and he wanted to continue mentoring them. And since he didn't have the day-to-day responsibility of the service and installation departments, he had the time to spend with the salespeople. As a result, profitable sales grew.

Yes, for the next two years profits did decline, because we had a huge overhead increase with the managers. It caused an increase in our overhead cost per hour. That overhead increase is now absorbed into the company operations, and our overhead cost per hour is now lower than it had been before we hired the managers. This happened because the number of field employees increased, so there were more field personnel to cover the total overhead.

We track activities each week through our weekly communications meeting, and the managers are running their departments profitably. The company is now over $5 million in sales and heading toward our $10 million goal.

Conclusion

||||||||||||||||||||||||||||||||||||||||||||||||||||||||||||||||||||||||||||||||

If you want to start and grow a business, then follow the rules of profit and wealth described in this book. I created these rules to help business owners achieve the goals and wealth they desire. Since 1981 I have been implementing them and refining them. They work for my business. They work for my clients' businesses. They will work for you. Just follow them.

Please create a recurring revenue stream for your business. Be creative. Offer your customers a reason to purchase from your company each month, each quarter, or each year. These customers become loyal customers who remain customers for many years and refer their friends and families to your company.

Recurring revenue builds profits and wealth. When it is time to pass your company to the next generation or sell it, you have something of value to sell. You have wealth and are rewarded for your years of hard work.

Get your financial statements on time every month. Then review them. They will tell you what is happening with your business. You will make better decisions using accurate data.

I wish you success and fulfillment of your goals and desires.

ACKNOWLEDGMENTS

This book would never have been written without you, my small business clients, over the past 36 years. Thank you for allowing me to help you grow profitably and build wealth. As one of you said, I have been responsible for many of the highest highs and lowest lows in your life. I hope there have been many more highs than lows for you.

Brenda Bethea has been my "right arm" for more than 29 years. She has participated in the growth, heard your stories, and been in the trenches with me for this entire journey.

I'm grateful to my parents, who guided my early years and helped shape the woman I have become. Although I didn't always appreciate your actions, you were always there to pick up the pieces when I made mistakes and cheer me on when I was working to achieve a goal.

To my late husband, Bob, who, during that last conversation we had, told me to "Do my thing." This book is a result of our conversation.

And finally to my daughter, Kate, your journey is under way. I hope that you find happiness and success. Use the stories in this book to help you build recurring revenue, profit, and wealth.

Thank you all. I love and appreciate you.

About the Author

Profitability Master Ruth King is president of Business Ventures Corporation. Ruth has a passion for helping small businesses get and stay profitable.

She is especially proud of one small business owner she helped climb out of a big hole. He started with a negative $400,000 net worth 15 years ago and is still in business today… profitably and with a positive net worth.

After 12 years on the road, doing 200 flights per year, she knew there had to be a better way to reach businesspeople who wanted to build their businesses and train their employees. She began training on the internet in 1998 and began the first television-like broadcasting in 2002. Her channels include www.hvacchannel.tv, 24/7/365 broadcasting on www.profitabilityrevolution.com, and others.

Ruth holds an MBA in finance from Georgia State University and bachelor's and master's degrees in chemical engineering from Tufts University and the University of Pennsylvania, respectively.

She started the Decatur, Georgia, branch of the Small Business Development Center in 1982. She also started the Women's Entrepreneurial Center and taught a year-long course for women who wanted to start their own businesses. This course was the foundation for one of the classes at the Women's Economic Development Authority in Atlanta, Georgia.

More recently Ruth was the instructor for \the Inner City Entrepreneur program in conjunction with the Small Business Administration. This 16-week course taught business owners with at least $400,000 in revenues (and many had over $1 million in revenues) how to grow to the next level. A large part of the curriculum was aimed at improving the financial knowledge of the business owners enrolled in the course.

Ruth is passionate about helping adults learn to read, photography, and marathon races (she has run 14, including two Boston Marathons). She helped start an adult literacy organization in 1986 that currently serves over 1,000 adults per year.

Her number one best-selling book, *The Courage to Be Profitable*, was named as one of the 37 books all startup businesses should read by London-based Fupping. She joins esteemed authors Napoleon Hill, Dale Carnegie, Stephen Covey, Richard Branson, and others on this list. *The Courage to Be Profitable* explains how to get and stay profitable in less than 30 minutes a month—in English rather than accounting babble. She is also the author of three other award-winning books: *The Ugly Truth about Cash*, *The Ugly Truth about Small Business*, and *The Ugly Truth about Managing People.* Go to www.ruthking.info or send an email to rking@ontheribbon.com to contact Ruth.

A Special Offer

Thank you for investing in this book! Get free online training!

As a thank you for investing in *Profit or Wealth?* you will receive free access to all of our online programs on sales, marketing, financials, and more on my website: www.profitabilityrevolution.com

To receive this access, create an account at www.profitabilityrevolution.com and add anything you want to your cart. Then at checkout, enter the coupon code "blackieripleybruno2019".

I hope these help you generate more profits and wealth.

CPSIA information can be obtained
at www.ICGtesting.com
Printed in the USA
JSHW022130140620
6209JS00004B/7